Robin Ryan has appeared on *Oprah, Dr. Phil, NBC Nightly News, Fox News,* CNN, CNBC and has made more than one thousand television and radio appearances. She is the best-selling author of seven books, including: *60 Seconds & You're Hired!; Winning Resumés,* 2nd edition; *Winning Cover Letters,* 2nd edition; and *What to Do with the Rest of Your Life.* She is the creator of the acclaimed audio and computer training programs, *Interview Advantage; Resumes and Cover Letters Creation Kit; The DreamMaker;* and *The Brand You Kit.*

Robin Ryan is an internationally syndicated career columnist and has been featured in or has published articles in: *Money, Newsweek, Fortune, Business Week, Working Woman, Cosmopolitan, Good Housekeeping, Glamour, Marie Clair,* and *Woman's Day.* She has also appeared on the pages of most major newspapers, including: *USA Today, The Wall Street Journal, The New York Times, Los Angeles Times, The Boston Globe,* and *Chicago Tribune.* More than one hundred Gannet newspapers carry her career column and she also regularly contributes articles to websites, including MSN, AOL, Career Builder, and HR.com.

Robin Ryan has spent a lifetime dedicated to helping people advance their careers. A licensed vocational counselor for more than twenty years, she has an active career-counseling practice where she offers both personal and telephone consultations to assist a nationwide list of clients. With fifteen years of hiring responsibility, Robin also teaches hiring, strengths identification/personal brand development, and career development seminars to employers, HR groups, executive teams, and employees.

A popular national speaker, Robin has motivated more than twelve hundred corporate, association, college, alumni, and professional groups and audiences through in-person programs, teleseminars, webinars, and elearning classes. She holds a master's degree in counseling and education from Suffolk University, a bachelor's degree in sociology from Boston College, and is the former director of counseling services at the University of Washington.

Robin Ryan contributes to the career success of millions every year. To learn more about her services and read more of her articles on advancing your career, visit **www.RobinRyan.com,** email **robinryan@aol.com,** or call **425.226.0414.**

Get her **free eNewsletter** of monthly career advice by signing up at **www.RobinRyan.com.**

ROBIN RYAN

SOARING

ON YOUR

STRENGTHS

Discover, Use, and Brand Your Best Self

for Career Success

Penguin Books

PENGUIN BOOKS
Published by the Penguin Group
Penguin Group (USA) Inc., 375 Hudson Street, New York,
New York 10014, U.S.A.
Penguin Group (Canada), 90 Eglinton Avenue East, Suite 700, Toronto,
Ontario, Canada M4P 2Y3 (a division of
Pearson Penguin Canada Inc.)
Penguin Books Ltd, 80 Strand, London WC2R 0RL, England
Penguin Ireland, 25 St Stephen's Green, Dublin 2, Ireland
(a division of Penguin Books Ltd)
Penguin Group (Australia), 250 Camberwell Road, Camberwell, Victoria
3124, Australia (a division of Pearson Australia GroupPty Ltd)
Penguin Books India Pvt Ltd, 11 Community Centre,
Panchsheel Park, New Delhi–110 017, India
Penguin Group (NZ), cnr Airborne and Rosedale Roads,
Albany, Auckland 1310, New Zealand (a division of Pearson
New Zealand Ltd)
Penguin Books (South Africa) (Pty) Ltd, 24 Sturdee Avenue,
Rosebank, Johannesburg 2196, South Africa

Penguin Books Ltd, Registered Offices:
80 Strand, London WC2R 0RL, England

First published in Penguin Books 2006

1   3   5   7   9   10   8   6   4   2

Copyright © Robin Ryan, 2006
All rights reserved

Mind Mapping is a registered trademark of the Buzan Organization

ISBN 0 14 30.3650 5

Printed in the United States of America
Set in Adobe Caslon and Trade Gothic
Designed by Judith Stagnitto Abbate/Abbate Design

For my beloved son, Jack,
who shows me daily that there is
a shining light inside each of us.

For my wonderful husband, Steven,
who has my deepest admiration for using his talents
to heal so many, and supporting me
with a love that makes me sparkle.

ACKNOWLEDGMENTS

My work rewards me in so many ways. Nothing beats the thrill I get when I see a client succeed. It's been a privilege to have worked with so many great people and played a small guiding role in their lives. I am grateful for the opportunity to help them and the chance to share their successes.

I am blessed to have a buddy like Dr. Gregg Jantz, who gives *so generously* and he's done nothing but inspire and encourage me and my work from the day we met.

A *big* thank you goes to Molly Lavik, a very talented marketing professor at Pepperdine University. She offered wonderful insights into the world of branding, along with contributing terrific ideas that significantly improved this book.

Many experts, executives, and human resource managers

offered insights that enriched this book. A few stand out that need special acknowledgment: Kenny Moore, who made me think in a new way; Tom McMahon, who shared his knowledge in his precious little free time; Ryan Hixenbaugh, whose knowledge of branding pushed me forward into these unknown territories; Mindy Howard, a brilliant CEO, author, and friend, who offered ideas and support; Rosemary Brown, Richard Lloyd, Cathy Joyce, and Tracy White, who all offered valuable comments on the idea.

I'm indebted to Dr. Henriette Klauser, who is exceptional in creating book proposals and improved mine. Nancy Atkins offered thorough administrative support on this book and made several conceptual improvements.

Sylva Coppock, who ran my office for the last three years, retired at the end of the writing of this book. She was the queen of assistants, extraordinarily talented, and I am lucky to have her on my team.

Every working mother needs reliable help and I have a gem in Patti Lowe, who is fabulous in the way she takes care of our family.

Jane von Mehren has risen to the top of the publishing field, yet she is still faithful in supporting all her authors and encouraging them. This book came about at her request and I am grateful for her wonderful, ongoing support of me and my work.

David Cashion became my working editor well into the game. Many of the significant improvements we made came from his suggestions. His outstanding strength is editing and this book greatly benefited from his talents.

Jane; David; Maureen Donnelly, who runs the book world's best publicity department; and the entire Penguin team represent the best publishing house any author could ever hope to work with. I am thankful for all you do for me and for helping my book get into the hands of readers who can benefit from it.

During the months while I was writing this book, I became seriously ill. Fortunately, a gifted surgeon and dedicated physician who truly cares about his patients took care of me. I offer a heartfelt thank you to Dr. Calvin Knapp.

Each day I thank God for my precious family. My husband, Steven Ryan, was terrific during this book project. He read this work, giving terrific suggestions and ideas and pointed out numerous ways to make my message better understood and succinct. Thanks so much for everything, Steven, especially for letting me make the house a mess for months as I researched and wrote this book.

My six-year-old son, Jack, was pretty understanding about the fact that his mama needed writing time. Still, his sweet interruptions always warmed my heart as only his laughter, smiles, and big squishy hugs can do. Thank you, my son, for being the sparkling, shimmering light in my life. I love you as I've loved no other.

Each of us receives a share of adversity and I faced some big challenges and despair when weeks of illness necessitated bed rest. During that time I was unable to think or concentrate, let alone write a book. Discouraged, I asked for God's help so I could complete my work. He sent friends, support, and gradual improvement in my health so I could get the book finished and, most important, He aided me in sharing this important message with the world.

CONTENTS

PART 4   IMPLEMENTING *BRAND YOU*

PART 5   CREATING YOUR FUTURE DESTINY

Keep interested in your own career, it is a real possession in the changing fortunes of time.

MAX EHRMANN, *DESIDERATA*

> *" Destiny is not a matter of chance, it is a matter of*
> *choice; it is not a thing to be waited for,*
> *it is a thing to be achieved. "*

WILLIAM JENNINGS BRYAN,
secretary of state during Woodrow Wilson's presidency

INTRODUCTION

oday's competitive and quickly changing work-place has altered the rules on how to get ahead. *Soaring on Your Strengths* offers a new career advancement method in this ever-shifting world. By establishing a career identity that uses your natural and best talents, you'll learn how to distinguish yourself from your peers, land more promotions, and obtain better raises, assignments, and dream jobs. You are about to create a career identity in the same way that a company creates a brand name for a product. The major difference is that in this case the product is *you*.

As a career counselor for more than twenty years, I've worked with thousands of clients just like you who aspired to a better life—and achieved it. After analyzing my clients' experiences, as well as gathering and analyzing information from endless human resource and hiring managers, CEOs, and top executives, I've learned what allows a person to advance his or her career, work in a job he or she loves, establish his or her true worth, and be highly paid. All of this has led me to write *Soaring on Your Strengths*.

Regardless of your current career situation, there's a section of this book tailored just for you. There is a special chapter on customizing *Brand You* to support whatever phase you are in: early career, midcareer, executive career, or the stage where you reinvent yourself. Each section includes precise details, action steps, and exercises to define your personal brand and career identity so that it's recognized by your boss, upper management, coworkers, and peers. In addition to the *Brand You* development program, you will learn how to create your own road map and implement your own action plan.

Most people learn best by hearing practical examples, so you'll benefit from the true stories of a number of my clients. (Throughout the book, though, names have been changed for privacy.) These client examples clearly illustrate how to apply the *Brand You* strategies and use this method in your own life to achieve greater success and prosperity. After all, you, too, have unique gifts, innate talents, and key strengths that will allow you to build a wonderful future, if you use them to the best of your ability.

It's time to take a closer look at the genuine, quality person you are, and to nurture your individual gifts so they'll blossom. As a result, you'll find greater rewards and meaning from the career you live. If you wish to excel, advance, earn more, and be happier, then read on. The answers lie ahead.

> *"People are definitely happier at work if they can utilize their best strengths on their job."*

THE DALAI LAMA,
author of *The Art of Happiness at Work*

PART 1

ESTABLISHING
YOUR CAREER IDENTITY

" Happiness depends upon ourselves. "

ARISTOTLE

CHAPTER 1

DISTINGUISH YOURSELF
FROM THE PACK

on't you want to be the best you that you can possibly be? Isn't your ultimate fantasy to have a career you love? A job where others recognize and praise your talents? A position where you are nicely rewarded in salary and perks?

That fantasy can quickly turn into reality if you are savvy enough to see that a new paradigm is sweeping through the workplace, one where employers are focusing on matching an employee's strengths to the job requirements for a particular position. It used to be that managers encouraged employees to focus on improving their weaknesses. Now the human resource trend is to develop and enhance natural strengths, since an employee using his or her inherent gifts is found to perform better on the tasks required by the job.

The number one *New York Times* best seller, *First, Break All the Rules* from the Gallup Poll study by Marcus Buckingham and Curt Coffman, cited more than 80,000 interviews to test the hypothesis of whether working on strengths betters your career, or if working on overcoming weaknesses will help you advance to a higher level. After examining why top managers excelled, the study decisively concluded that one reason stood out—successful managers consistently used their strengths.

For their book *The 5 Patterns of Extraordinary Careers* James Citrin and Richard Smith conducted thousands of interviews and discovered that extraordinary executives worked their way up by playing to their strengths and following their passion.

And a recent issue of *Employment Management Today,* a trade journal of the Society for Human Resource Management, discussed a growing trend to accent the positive in employees and match their strengths to their jobs. Employment studies cited by the article revealed that many people are misemployed, meaning they are not well matched by personality or interest in their current positions.

Unfortunately, and for too long, our society has been focused on thinking that attempting to fix weaknesses is what management of employees is all about. *Not true!* Research shows that people who are allowed to use their strengths perform their very best each day and are much more successful and productive on the job. This approach results in a win-win situation—employers get more engaged and productive workers, while the employee gets a job that's rewarding and fulfilling.

YOUR CAREER IDENTITY

IF YOUR BOSS or a potential manager asked what you excel at doing, could you quickly state what your key strengths are? Do you know what your career identity is? Not your job title, but your *career identity*, that unique reputation you have among bosses, colleagues, and other employees.

If you don't have an answer that automatically rolls off your tongue, you are not alone. Most people haven't given much thought to how they are perceived at work. But everyone needs to think about that question if they wish to become the best they can be and get greater joy, better rewards, and increased personal satisfaction from their jobs.

A job title is a title, but it is *not* who you are when we refer to your personal career identity. Your career identity is your professional reputation, and it is also known as your *personal brand.* It reflects other people's opinion of you as a worker, the associations they make when they think about you, and what you do or don't do well. Your *personal brand,* which we refer to as *Brand You,* communicates your career identity to the world.

Throughout your professional life, you must continually define and promote your personal brand in order to keep it vibrant and to distinguish yourself in the workplace. *Soaring on Your Strengths* is a crash course that will teach you how to reinvent yourself into *the best you that you can possibly be.* Through personal branding, you will learn to set yourself apart by emphasizing your talents in a way that showcases what is distinctive about you. You can develop a mark of excellence that reflects your own unique talents and abilities in the tasks or activities that you do best. People who display a great personal brand find it is the very reason for their success. Others will never advance until they learn how to develop the best part of themselves—their natural gifts.

SO WHAT IS *BRAND YOU?*

YOUR CAREER IDENTITY is not some slick piece of advertising. *Brand You* is based on the authentic, talented, and genuinely unique and special person you are. It is *not* phony, conceited, or exaggerated, nor is it a trick or fleeting fad. The components of *Brand You* are the essence of you as a person. They include your work strengths, your image, your passion, your personality traits, and others' perceptions of you applied in a work environment that enhances your productivity.

There's quite a crowd of human beings out there competing for the job or promotion you'd like to get. To stand out means utilizing *Brand You* especially when almost everyone else is largely undefined. Advancing your personal brand is the most effective career development strategy you can implement. So consider how you want to be thought of by your employer or supervisor. Do you want her to see you as just plain, ordinary, average? The answer is an emphatic *no* if you care about promotions, better jobs, challenging assignments, and making more money.

WORK SMART: USE YOUR GIFTS

NOT EVERYBODY IS created equal. This is a fact of life. Some people are perceived to be better than others at the tasks the job requires, and it is essential that you be seen as the one who is better able to perform in today's workplace.

Whether you choose to acknowledge it or not, *each person already is a brand,* though most people do a very poor job of managing their professional identity and reputation. How would you describe yours? Is it highly valued and continuously recognized? Or is your career identity nondescript, unknown, and unrecognized? Is it one that does not serve you well in today's workplace? These are critical questions you need to ask and answer.

As you shape your career identity into one that is highly valued and well rewarded by employers, you'll travel down a road on which you'll learn—through examples drawn from the experiences of my former career counseling clients—how to be successful by more clearly defining and communicating your personal brand. The results they achieved and results you can achieve for yourself include the following:

- fast-track promotions
- power and control in directing your career
- greater autonomy in your work duties
- higher salary and nicer perks
- better assignments
- flexible work schedules
- greater joy, satisfaction, and fulfillment from your job

By the end of this book, you will possess a clearly defined career identity, referred to as *Brand You.* No matter where you are in your career—beginning, middle, or senior level, or if you are changing careers or reinventing yourself—you'll have a game plan for your future. You will know how to self-promote and self-market successfully to become the very best you can be. By correctly communicating *Brand You* to bosses, potential employers, and coworkers, you can remain a viable worker longer and be retained when others are downsized. Your life will improve as you are *actively* recruited for promotions, special projects, and new positions.

YOUR REFERENCES MATTER MORE THAN YOUR RESUMÉ

AS THE CEO of your own personal brand, your job is to actively build and shape your reputation into a very appealing one. In today's complex workplace, *it is no longer your resume that's the most powerful tool in your career arsenal, it is your references.* It's the comments, endorsements, and recommendations from past bosses, colleagues, and coworkers that define your career reputation. In other words, the *brand you* have created for yourself. We see this played out daily as employers seeking to hire rely heavily on referrals. In fact during the last year, 63% of all jobs were found through using contacts (introductions and referrals), according to the Department of Labor.

References are not only the most influential factor in who gets promoted or hired, they also impact your perceived value and worth as a worker. When someone labels you as being really good that usually translates into a company's willingness to pay you a higher salary to ensure you remain on their team, or, if you are looking for a new position, that you will *join* their team. Cultivating and maintaining good work relationships where others clearly know your strengths becomes a major asset to you for achieving greater success.

You can recession proof yourself, and find a lifetime of good jobs and security by differentiating yourself from the competition who are vying for the promotion or new job you want.

CAN YOU DO THIS?

BRAND YOU TAKES work, time, and energy. But it knows no limitation and excludes no field or industry. You can be a distinguished chef, accountant, mechanic, teacher, salesman, hairstylist, banker, manager, or CEO. In any career you can become the cream that rises to the top by distinguishing your strengths and establishing your uniqueness.

Unfortunately, many of today's workers are unwilling to take the time to invest in themselves in order to excel. According to a recent Society for Human Resource Management survey, 70% of the workforce is comprised of disengaged workers. Most employees are content to be average. They have potential, but in their unpolished, unbranded state they, like rough uncut diamonds, have little value. It certainly takes more effort to become good—very good—at something. Many refuse to put in the effort, so greater success eludes them. And that's actually good news for you. If you are the one who puts in something extra, you are also the one who will have a better chance to get ahead and prosper.

This personal brand process isn't just for the lucky, the exceptionally talented, or the smartest people in the workplace. And you don't need a diploma from a prestigious college or numerous professional degrees. You do need ambition, self-respect, drive, a love of learning, and a success-driven, results-oriented, CAN-DO attitude to better define your own unique career identity.

In summary, a new paradigm has happened in the workplace where careers are advanced by memorable individuals who rely on and use their strengths at work. And with this book you'll learn how *Brand You:*

- helps you believe in yourself
- lets others know your perceived value
- gets you credit for your accomplishments
- acknowledges and develops your talents
- is memorable
- is proactive, with a positive can-do attitude
- continually learns and embraces new ideas

If you raise the bar on your goals and dreams and make happiness the ultimate metric, you can take complete responsibility for your success. Inside you lie all the talents you need to flourish and prosper. Using your innate strengths guarantees that you can successfully improve, advance, or jump-start your career.

A high school student who dreamed of a singing career got a C in music. His teacher told him, "Boy, you just can't sing. You better find another way to make a living because singing songs obviously won't be it." Elvis Presley chose not to listen.

CHAPTER 2

DISCOVER YOUR OWN UNIQUE GENIUS

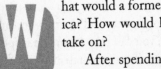hat would a former monk do in corporate America? How would he fit in? What job would he take on?

After spending fifteen years in a monastery, Kenny Moore joined KeySpan, a *Fortune* 500 company. Moore uniquely defines his job there by saying, "My role is to share my gifts and talents." However, if you look him up in the company's directory, you'll find his title is director of human resources and corporate ombudsman. He is also the coauthor, along with KeySpan CEO Robert Catell, of an insightful book entitled, *The CEO and the Monk*.

An exceptional individual, Kenny Moore has a theological point of view about the inner meaning of work. During our extensive interview he said, "True happiness is intimately connected to our vocational calling. Gifts are given both for the individual and the collective common good. Every person has gifts, but the talents bestowed on you come with a responsibility." The HR director added, "Whatever gifts you have, you can't hide—you must use them."

Desire for happiness is what drives every human—it's a universal motivation. We've seen corporate America degrade the person, point out defects, and rarely emphasize strengths, Moore explains. "I trip over talented people who aren't highly successful or highly educated, yet each has tremendous talents and potential."

This human resources director has spent twenty-one years in a major organization where he's advised many people on their career paths. With the inner philosophical thoughts of a meditative monk, he offers some excellent advice on developing an individual brand. Moore suggests, "Ask yourself what makes you come alive, and then go and do that. When you answer your vocational calling, and go out and do what makes you come alive, the world will assist you, and you will find true happiness."

The value you possess is independent of the company or organization you work for. Your worth is not measured by your title, position, power, or salary. Most people internalize what the outside world says, but *personal power*—not status, not position—is personal. Your power *is* inside you. Your personal banner needs to be: I HAVE VALUE! I HAVE WORTH! HOW DARE ANYONE TELL ME I'M WORTHLESS?

Never forget that you control your own personal power, create your own happiness, and choose whether or not to use your talents. The first step of *Brand You* really starts with your inner belief and an attitude that you are special, possess natural gifts, and have great value to offer the world.

Every person has been given their own destiny. Some choose to use their talents, while others ignore and waste them, living life unfulfilled and often unrewarded. Sadly, too many people don't see how great they could be. So many don't feel special. They reinforce these confidence-dooming thoughts with self-defeating talk. Even outwardly successful people—managers, directors, and top executives—can suffer from doubts or the imposter complex. Too many think, "I'm faking it. I'm really not that good." Others think, "I'm just average, there's nothing special about me." *But they are wrong.* It is their negative self-talk that creates the doubts and devalues what is unique or special about them.

Each and every single person alive has unique and valuable strengths. Taking notice of a genetic anomaly can shed some light on this. My brothers, Rich and Dave, are identical twins, and since they *look* just alike, many conclude they *are* alike. Because of their physical resemblance and similar mannerisms, and the fact that they both work in the film industry, they do seem to be just alike. Yet when you get to know them, you discover each twin has his own set of distinctive and unique talents.

Rich has terrific business management, budgeting, finance, and superior negotiating skills. Likeable with a terrific mind for making deals, he's analytical and a great problem solver. A successful film producer, he has excelled and gone a long way relying on his talents.

Dave has little natural business management strength. His gifts lie in being a sensitive and intuitive person, a creative storyteller and writer. He can envision movie scenes, stage them so they look great on film, and then direct the actors to capture the essence of the character. Dave has written more than a dozen screenplays with half of those already made into movies and another in line for production.

Each identical twin developed his own unique genius, and

followed his passion. If two people with exactly the same genetic materials and cultural background can possess and apply their talents differently, this only proves that each of us truly possesses a unique genius.

Sometimes, however, it takes a career counseling session for someone to understand his special qualities and understand the power of *Brand You*.

One of my clients worked for eBay and longed to land a coveted promotion. The major problem was figuring out how to stand out in a place full of type A achievers. The corporate culture inside eBay is intense—you are either highly productive and produce great results or you wash out and are gone. There's no in-between. This is a competitive environment where people want to be stars and set the world on fire.

John was a project manager and our first step was to examine his key strengths and core competencies. Like many successful people, John had a hard time acknowledging the importance of his talents or accomplishments. In the area of worth, he devalued himself and his talents, skills, and achievements. Our first task was to identify his unique brand, and to place a higher value on his proven talents.

We outlined what his key strengths were:

- project management
  - handles multiple complex projects simultaneously
  - delivers on time
- leadership
  - builds motivated and productive teams
  - is a strong mentoring coach
  - manages large projects with little or no supervision
- strategic planner
  - global thinker
  - analytical thinker
  - great organizational skills

- communication skills
  - consensus builder across multifunctional teams
  - resourceful problem solver
- persuasive skills
  - ensures that tasks and priorities are met

After a revealing session, we crafted a new resumé that clearly emphasized John's strengths, competencies, and past accomplishments. During his crucial promotion interview, John was able to stress that he was a proven leader with solid project management skills and was a terrific problem solver. With a quiet but open style, he illustrated that he had excellent analytical, organizational, developmental, and strategic planning abilities. He had been recognized by his boss on several occasions for his strong interpersonal communication and persuasive talents, his leadership strengths, his effectiveness in building consensus, and his ability to regularly meet goals and deadlines. He was also known for introducing innovative and creative solutions to difficult problems and excelling in mentoring team members and building productive relationships with everyone he encountered. What he did in both his resumé and interviews was to emphasize his personal brand. He illustrated his ability to prioritize tasks, as well as his resourceful way of meeting challenges, which were acknowledged by his boss. John got the promotion, and eBay gave him a handsome raise along with his new job title.

John had never thought about himself as a brand. Most people don't. He hadn't realized the importance of differentiating and marketing himself until he wanted the promotion. He worked hard, loved what he did, and believed it was enough. "Doing a job well is innate and instinctive for me," he'd said. Still, he acknowledged that it's only when others higher up are familiar with you and recognize your talents, strengths, and contributions, that your perceived value increases.

You, too, need a clear picture of who you are. Begin from

where you are right now. It doesn't matter if you're at the beginning or middle or near the top of your career. It doesn't matter if you wish to remain in the same field, change industries, or even redefine yourself and change careers. It doesn't matter what perceived obstacles you think you face—job loss, age, handicap, lack of or too much experience—these are only challenges that need to be overcome. What does matter is that if you wish to forge a different path or excel in the current one, it is *always possible* to build greater success and satisfaction into your life.

You're now going to do some important self-assessment. This is the foundation—determining your strengths, values, passions, competencies—on which you are going to build and advance your career. These assessment questions will guide you toward your final definition of *Brand You*, so answer honestly, accurately, and don't undervalue yourself.

As a starting point, write a brief paragraph stating what is unique and special about you. If you find this challenging then think back to when you were an adolescent or teen. Even then, your key natural strengths were evident. For example, were you a debater, a wizard at math, a terrific speller, or always on the computer? Were you the Dear Abby, constantly advising your friends? Maybe you were more mechanically inclined, fixing things. Try to recall your gifts, bearing in mind that these talents are probably still true today.

The next exercise can give you a realistic picture of how you are perceived. Ask others to assess you since your *Brand You* career identity is shaped by others' perceptions of you. Therefore, this is an important exercise to help get an accurate self-assessment. Ask three people who are familiar with your work to tell you what they think you are good at. Record their responses.

PERSON #1

PERSON #2

PERSON #3

Don't be tempted to skip this part of the assessment. It's critical to hear and most important, understand, how others see you. You might be pleasantly surprised by the mention of innate gifts you, too, often just take for granted.

Next, state how you'd like to be perceived by your boss and upper management.

BRAND COMPONENTS

IN THE SECTIONS that follow, you will be introduced to the key concepts that will help define your personal brand. These components include:

Brand Equity—your notable strengths
Brand Advantage—your core competency

Brand Passion—your utmost interests, associated with the question, "What was I born to do?"

Brand Values—what you care most about

Brand Essence—the personality traits that make you distinctively you

Brand Image—your presentation and appearance to the outside world

Brand Reputation—how others see you and what they say about you

Add all these components together and you have *Brand You,* the unique genius that is distinctly your own. Couple that with a work environment that allows you to flourish, and the sky's the limit for your success, and most important, for your personal happiness at work.

BRAND EQUITY—TALENTS AND STRENGTHS

YOUR TALENTS AND strengths make up your Brand Equity. This is the foundation of *Brand You.* You must spend some time carefully considering all you do. Don't devalue yourself, but instead, be positive and acknowledge your strengths.

So what are your talents? Your natural God-given gifts? You must first be clear on what your strengths are so you can develop them to advance your career. Let's consider them all. Since many people get more criticism on what they don't do well, here's a brief list to get your brain working on assessing the positive talents you do exhibit.

Strengths

active listener
analytical
artistic
building/constructing
classifying data and
information
coaching and consulting
conducting research
coordinating projects

counseling
creativity
critique or review others'
    work
customer service
debating
decision-making
delegating tasks
design
detail-oriented
drawing
editing
entertaining/humorous
establishing priorities
estimating
event planning
facilitating meetings
flair for color/design
fluent in another language
fundraising
global thinking
handling complaints
highly imaginative
implementing ideas
initiating change
inspection of physical
    objects
interpersonal skills
interpreting data
investigative powers
leadership ability
listening perceptively

mathematical skills
mediation
methodical
motivating and inspiring
    others
negotiation skills
organizing workflow
persuasive, able to
    influence others
plan large-scale projects or
    designs
preparing reports
promoting goods and
    services
providing social services
public speaking
quality improvement
reasoning capabilities
record keeping
repairing equipment
scheduling
self-motivated
selling products or services
statistics
strategic planning
systematizing
team building
verbal communication
    skills
visualization
word-processing skills
writing skills

There are hundreds more talents that aren't listed so if you think of some that aren't on this list, feel free to add them.

Create a list of your key strengths and write them below.

1.

2.

3.

4.

5.

6.

7.

8.

9.

10.

You've completed the hardest part. You've considered various tasks and skills to determine the numerous abilities you do possess. Even if you are just beginning your career, your strengths are innate and they've been displayed in your earlier activities. They could include natural sales or persuasive skills or artistic ability with color, clothes, or design. And for those who are further along in their careers, consider strengths you've used before, even many years ago, which can be redeveloped or used to advance you now. We have our talents from birth, and yours are apparent; they just need to be recognized, more clearly defined, and valued in the way they should be.

Using your key strengths in an area you dislike or are only mildly interested in will not allow you to be the best you can be. It is uniting your soul's passion with your vocational talents that gives you a personal brand that radiates enthusiasm. Your passion ignites your interest to keep pursuing knowledge and new training in order to become excellent at what you do. It fuels your brand so don't go to work without it.

BRAND ADVANTAGE—
YOUR CORE COMPETENCY

YOU HAVE SEVERAL talents and strengths. Some you have mastered better than others. Typically there are a few strengths that you perform *really* well. You know it. Others point it out to you. You may hear a compliment such as "great presentation" from your boss, coworkers, or colleagues frequently. Your family or friends have mentioned it to you. You may have won awards or some recognition for your skill. Your core competencies are noticed and recognized by others. Anything can be a core competency—but it is typically the strength that is often the top one (or ones) that people acknowledge about you.

For example, Laura was everyone's favorite event organizer. She was a true master at getting others to do whatever needed to be done. She planned major school or community events, always creating the best one the organization had ever had. She would plan giant charity events and raise hundreds of thousands of dollars, bettering the total every year. Laura was a master planner yet her true core competency was being a terrific manager who could recruit top talent to do what needed to be done. When it was time for publicity, she would recruit a TV anchor to help. When the newsletter needed writing, an accomplished book author was tapped. When large financial donations were necessary, she would go to the wealthiest patrons and come back with a check that featured a lot of zeroes. Her core competency was not being a good events planner, it was her strength in *recruiting the right person to do what she needed done, when she needed it, who would do it very well.*

In another example, Tony learned to ice skate at his daddy's knee—literally. He was only eighteen months old when his father laced up his skates and he hit the ice for the first time. He displayed a natural gift from day one. Tony grew up eating, sleeping, and breathing ice skating and hockey and eventually became a superstar player for his high school team and turned pro immediately thereafter. He played for the Canadian Maple Leafs and a few other national hockey teams. He had a long victorious career, but as with all professional athletes, the career comes to an end sooner than later. Many former pros turn to coaching, mostly for college or pro teams, but Tony had a core competency that was a bit different. He most enjoyed sharing the passion and skill he'd acquired for his favorite sport with very young kids. Tony leads several beginning hockey programs and offers one-on-one skating lessons. In fact, he's developed the reputation of being the top kid's ice skating instructor in his area. He systematically teaches children in a way that builds their confidence and makes them depend on their own self to master staying up on the ice. Tony's teaching method seems to be uniquely his. He offers a mix of encouragement and discipline. His approach works—he's taught more than a hundred kids who went on to play professional hockey, and nearly a thousand kids who just had fun skating around the rink and whacking a hockey puck. I've witnessed Tony in action, and I'd agree he is a fantastic teacher. His core competency is *teaching ice skating and hockey, motivating young boys and girls.*

Sometimes a person may have two or even three core competencies—things they have mastered to be the best at. Now consider what do you do best.

Write down exactly what your core competency or competencies are.

BRAND PASSION—THE DRIVE INSIDE

PEOPLE WHO HAVE successfully defined their personal brand all say, "I was born to do this." And they were. They have tapped into their own genius, their own talents, and are developing them to the fullest.

Everyday you meet people who were born to their vocation. Kristy Renkert left a better paying job to teach preschool. In a room full of three- and four-year-olds, she thrives on their energy and curiosity, and she finds that the hours fly by. She says, "I was born to do just this. I love shaping the minds of these little kiddos as they are beginning to develop and explore the world." Show up at her classroom door any morning and you'll feel overwhelmed with the noise, the chaos, and the energy of those young people. Few of us would say we were born to face that day after day, and yet Kristy wakes up happy that it's her job, knowing she's doing exactly what she was meant to.

> Let's assess your passion. Pay attention to that feeling of elation you experience when you do something well. It's this internal recognition that lets you know you have found your real purpose in life.
>
> If you could do anything, what would it be?
>
>
>
> What are the big dreams that you want to achieve in your lifetime?

What achievements and talents are you most proud of?

What do you feel you were born to do?

Write down one of your dreams you want to accomplish in the next year or two.

List all the action steps that you must take to make this dream come true. (Include any sacrifices you must make or obstacles to overcome.)

At work, define what you are most productive at. Note what makes you feel terrific (for example, handling challenges, completing a project, helping others, writing an article, selling to a new customer, receiving financial reward, and so on).

In what skills have you excelled in the past?

What have others praised you for?

How will you know when you've achieved success? (Be specific.)

What is your mission, your fate, your destiny?

You must be determined and committed to your own success. Let this be your mantra:

This work means enough to me,
to make me do whatever is necessary,
to achieve it.

Dreams are only wishes without the action steps. Commitment turns dreams into goals and gives fuel to the actions that make the dreams become reality.

BRAND VALUES—BE TRUE TO YOURSELF

OUR VALUES OFTEN shift or change over our lifetimes. Inner meaning is derived from your own individual values. But it's easy to get distracted by other people's goals for you. Too many of us choose careers to please our parents or a spouse. Years are wasted because someone other than you decided what you should do with your life. You'll never be truly happy living out someone else's expectations.

As you develop *Brand You*, you need to clearly focus on your own ambition and define your goals. Determine what motivates you. For some people, upward promotions, important titles, power, and big salaries compel and define success. For

others, helping to care for someone who is ill or injured, or being involved in the political process, might matter most. Your
definition of success will be as individual and as unique as
you are.

Look around and you'll see evidence every day of people
living their values. My family moved recently and the moving
company sent Glen to help us. He was a jolly guy who truly enjoyed the whole process. I found this astonishing because I
hate moving. Yet I learned from Glen that he had a talent for
packing and safely transporting all types of belongings and he
enjoyed helping clients empty one house and settle into another. He told me, "Nothing is better than loading the truck
and then transforming an empty shell of a house by filling it
with your belongings to make it your new home. I love the
sense of accomplishment at the end of the day." He was excellent at what he did—careful and speedy. That was his brand.
He came highly recommended to us and we've since recommended him to others. Why? Because he was good! He also
told me that he made a great living as a mover. He did not own
the company and he didn't own the truck. He just earned
wages from his labor and said he made more than $100,000 a
year doing what he loves. Glen stayed true to himself and pros-
pered from it.

You must be in sync and congruent with your own personal
value system. Using your talents and instincts—doing whatever
it is you do—must truly matter. You take great pride in it and
feel your endeavors are worthwhile.

You can choose how you use your natural talents. Perhaps
you have chosen a path and now you find you just don't like it.
You can select another profession. If you are already successful,
you have the power to become an even greater success. You
could create a legacy, make a significant difference, and leave
something behind of great value. Ultimately, the consequences
of each of your past goals and intentions brought actions and

choices that created the life that you are currently living. Make a conscious decision that you are willing to accept responsibility for living the life that you want to live, one that's in line with what you value, regardless of what anybody else thinks. Begin implementing changes today.

Briefly note what kinds of things matter to you the most.

How could you make a difference?

BRAND ESSENCE—THE TRAITS THAT MAKE YOU—YOU!

YOU WERE BORN with inherent personality traits. Established in childhood, your basic personality remains fairly constant throughout your entire life. It directs the way you act and think. Personality traits are the distinguishing qualities that differentiate you from others. They establish your identity and how you express that identity to the outside world. They are responsible for your habits, comfort zones, quirks, and behavioral patterns.

As you define *Brand You*, understand that your personality's inherent traits guide your life's direction and influence what you become. They affect your self-image, self-esteem, self-confidence, and self-worth. They motivate you, create your irritations, and control stress and how that stress affects you.

According to most personality theories, we each have within our own personality type both strengths and weaknesses. These are primarily determined by the genetic, neurological hard wiring found within our brain. Whereas one person is a wizard with computers, another who is not wired for understanding these complex systems and how computers work, finds the technology to be mind-boggling. The more you function within your inherent strengths, psychologists say, the stronger and more confident you become, the better your sense of reality, and the more control you have over your life. Strengths (the core of *Brand You*) put you in a stronger position to take advantage of and maximize the opportunities that life sets before you, and equips you to make the choices that will create the life you want.

However, if you function outside your core competencies, and work from your weaknesses, over time you become emotionally drained, mentally confused, and experience stress-related aches, pains, and other physical discomforts. Your life feels as if it is out of control, and you have a strong sense of being detached from its pleasures. Emotionally numbed, your thinking becomes fuzzy. Apathy results in dissatisfaction with your job, and prevents you from getting where you want to go.

Only you can change a negative situation to a more positive one. By respecting and using your strengths and personality traits to your advantage, you'll excel and be happier than you believed possible.

Here are some common personality descriptors to get you thinking:

abrasive

adventuresome

aggressive

aloof

altruistic

ambiguous

ambitious

analytical

artistic

blunt

boisterous

caring

charismatic

cheerful

compassionate

considerate

controlling

creative

decisive

dedicated

demanding

dependable

down-to-earth

driven

dynamic

easygoing

energetic

enthusiastic

funny

generous

grumpy

helpful

impatient

innovative

intolerant

jaded

kind

loyal

manipulative

needy

nice

opinionated

perfectionist

practical

proud

resourceful

responsible

self-centered

self-confident

self-serving

sensitive

shrewd

shy

straightforward

sweet

tactful

thoughtful

tidy

trustworthy

vivacious

List five of your more dominant personality traits.

1.

2.

3.

4.

5.

You cannot change the basic core of your personality. It's important to acknowledge who you are, and what your dominant traits are and play to your strengths. This assessment helps you better understand how others react to you and acknowledge that there are things that would be very difficult to change or that you simply can't change.

BRAND IMAGE—THE RIGHT APPEARANCE

AN AMBITIOUS WOMAN who dreamed of a TV anchor job, was thrilled to be hired by CNN. Her joy was short-lived however, when the company president banned her from doing on-air news, stating she had an irritating voice. Not willing to let her dream die, she got a voice coach and today Katie Couric hosts NBC's *Today* show and interviews people from all around the world.

It's a shame that bad first impressions are so difficult to overcome. Too many managers and senior executives tell me that they didn't promote somebody or they didn't select a candidate because they felt the person just didn't project the kind of image that the company wants its team to portray.

Your appearance and the way you present yourself are a part of your brand. Image has become a more complex issue in recent years because employers have found that casual dress has been sliding into downright sloppy. It's wise to always have a professional look at work and at work-related functions. Using your assets and presenting the best possible image of yourself can be a winning combination.

Just as Katie Couric found it necessary to address her on-air effectiveness, you, too, may need to review how you present yourself and possibly make improvements.

Go to a full-length mirror the next time you leave for work (or for a job interview). Take a serious look. How would you define your personal style and dress? Think of how your boss, his supervisor, and those higher up in the company dress. Are they formal or informal? Do they dress up for clients and big meetings? What image do they project? If you hope to move up, keep in mind that you need to *look like you fit in* with the upper management team.

> List ten qualities, attributes, or personality traits that you like about yourself or that others compliment you on. Now is not the time to be humble. For example, you can refer to physical attributes like great smile, athletic, or qualities such as snazzy dresser, friendly, and so on.
>
> 1.
> 2.
> 3.
> 4.
> 5.
> 6.
> 7.
> 8.
> 9.
> 10.

Your image is more than just external trappings—it's also how you project yourself and how you behave. Your movements, stance, gestures, communication style, and vocal intonation are all a part of how you are perceived.

Some often-forgotten keys that you either want to incorporate into your personal style, or simply remember to use include the following:

- **Sound positive.** Vary the pace and tone, be expressive, speak clearly, and *smile*.
- **Maintain eye contact.** This is one of the easiest ways to engage a person.
- **Actively listen and show interest.** People always want to be noticed and to feel appreciated.
- **Make small talk.** Inquire about the other person's life, interests, or family.
- **Pay attention to your grooming and hygiene.** It's more important than you think.
- **Be conscious of controlling nervous habits.** Don't fidget, play with your hair, tap your pen, wring your hands, and so forth. These habits are very distracting and off-putting.
- **Pay attention to the message you are sending with your nonverbal communication cues.** People are often interpreted and defined by their nonverbal cues and communication. For example, be aware of whether you are frowning or nodding your head in acceptance of what others are saying to you.
- **Speak up and offer your opinions.** Showing initiative is an asset, but think before you speak. There are times in a professional environment when saying what immediately comes to mind may not be the best avenue to endear yourself to others. Know when you should take the initiative to bring something up and when it's appropriate to bite your tongue.

To master your presentation to others, I can't stress enough how important it is to develop the composure to look people in the eye when communicating with them. Too often when people feel nervous, stressed, or intimidated they look everywhere except at the person they're talking to. If you do that, you won't come across as confident and you won't connect with the person you are talking to. Not only is this important in job interviews, it's important in your day-to-day work life. Many people don't realize it, but when they are talking in a business situation (such as to a senior executive or in a presentation, interview, or meeting) they're often looking at the ceiling, their notes, their hands—basically anywhere except the most important spot: directly into the eyes of the person they are addressing.

Where there is energy and enthusiasm, there is life! Ever wonder why so many people adore little children? They are full of life. They are so active, with so much energy. They smile and laugh out loud. There's absolute glee on a child's face and a sparkle in his eyes when he looks at you. Children are excited and enthusiastic about everything they see and do. When a small child smiles at you, you immediately have to smile back. Learn from kids that one of your best assets is your smile. You'll seem more approachable, friendlier, and more positive if you smile. Not smiling is one of the biggest mistakes people make in their job interview. Nervous candidates turn into robots, unable to smile. When you smile it's not just with your mouth. Your eyes twinkle, your voice radiates warmth, and joy is conveyed by your body language. A smile is a force that attracts others to you.

I'll discuss in more detail exactly what you can do to solidify or improve your Brand Image in chapter nine.

BRAND REPUTATION— HOW OTHERS SEE YOU

IRONICALLY, MOST OF us do not see ourselves as others do. A few think they are greater, better, or more gifted than they really are, but too often, many people actual view themselves in a devaluing light. They don't own their gifts and they rarely take the well-deserved credit for their accomplishments. This belief system often stems from how our families raised us. Many well-meaning parents teach their children that to be more humble is a virtue. In fact, this was Darren's problem. A director of finance with an MBA, he had a very hard time "selling himself." He wanted to step up and land a promotion, so he became a client of mine. But Darren continually downplayed his own accomplishments. He told me, "Financial analysis is a breeze; anyone can do what I do," and he believed that to be the truth. "Really?" I questioned. Everyone could *not* do exactly what he did. In fact, very few could. But Darren felt if he was capable of it, then it was no big deal. He was denying his own unique genius even when it was staring him right in the face. Past performance reviews had always been stellar, but his current boss seemed to not want to listen to Darren and his recommendations. That fostered Darren's internal belief that he wasn't doing anything special and wasn't that good. I disagreed with this client's self-perception, so I had him interview former bosses who gave him an earful of just how well thought of and good he really was.

The "devaluing himself" mind-set was holding him back. Yet the truth—that he was very good at financial analysis—was digested slowly. Once he processed it and we worked on changing his self-image, he was better able to discuss and take credit for his talents and accomplishments. The revelation worked its magic. Darren began to verbalize his strengths and core competencies and convinced a *Fortune* 500 company that he was a great fit for a VP job. Indeed, once he acknowledged his unique genius, he got that long-sought-after promotion.

Marilyn suffered from a related malady I call *the imposter complex*, a fear of others' uncovering that you're just not that good at whatever it is you do. A physician, Marilyn had returned to school and obtained an MBA since she had a natural aptitude for running the business side of medicine. She quickly made a reputation for herself as an outstanding medical director. She came to see me when three potential employers were wooing her to join their particular organization. Marilyn confessed to me that she was afraid that she wasn't as good as others might think. She feared if she took the new job she'd fail. The imposter complex needed dispelling. With some solid confidence building and after reviewing her past accomplishments, she took a new attitude into salary negotiations and got a better deal for herself than she ever dreamed possible.

Write out what you think your Brand Reputation is.

Since our perception of ourselves might vary from the world's, you need to question your associates to determine what, exactly, they think you are good at. What is your career identity and reputation according to them? You need to hear the good, the bad, and the mediocre. Or worse yet, the nondescript, when they don't say much at all. That's not a positive thing since your career advancement often depends on referrals for special assignments, promotions, and moves up the ladder. Your career identity is defined by what others think and say about you. You must know what that is. *Ask!* Do not skip this task since it is the essential foundation of *Brand You.*

To learn what others think, begin by reviewing past work evaluations, letters of recommendation, recognitions, and awards received to see if there is a consistent theme.

What are the noted strengths? Weaknesses? Memorable comments? Note these.

Next, actually interview a few people who have worked with you—bosses, coworkers, other colleagues, association members. What do they say?

Ask your family and close friends. What do they say?

Write out your brand reputation based on exactly what others have told you.

Do your opinion and the opinions of others match? If you said yes, terrific, you are well on your way. If you said no, then you need to examine what strengths or talents you need to better own. You must now, and from every day hereafter, take credit for your career accomplishments. You must begin to see yourself as others do. After all, it is others who recommend you for a new job, or a promotion, or a special assignment. And hiring managers pay a great deal of attention to the words from whoever is making the reference or referral. It's through their recommendations and references that they become your champion in the workplace, offering better jobs and much bigger salaries. If you suffer from devaluing yourself, then create a list of affirmations and begin the confidence building. If you overestimated your talents, work on mastering them to a realistic level. In the end, it is not our own opinions, but it is what others say about you and your talents, coupled with your track record, that will allow you—and your career—to grow and prosper.

In this chapter, we've looked at the components that define and make up your personal brand. They include the following:

- talents—natural gifts
- work strengths—core competencies applied on the job
- passion and top interests
- valuing what you do as important and meaningful
- personality traits that make you *you*
- image and outward appearance

All of these things are involved in defining the unique essence that is you.

In the chapters that follow you will get specific instructions on creating your personal brand, depending on your career stage: early, middle, executive, or reinventing yourself. You'll narrow down all of the *Brand You* components mentioned in this chapter.

You've already done some key personal assessment to better define your Brand Equity, Brand Advantage, Brand Passion, Brand Values, Brand Essence, Brand Reputation, and Brand Image. It should become clearer what your career identity is as you define the unique genius within.

Jay Leno recently said it best when he proclaimed, "Of all my relatives, I like me best." Indeed, you must be the first person to see the value you bring to the world. Self-acceptance and inner appreciation are the cornerstones of *Brand You*.

> " *I walked for miles along the beach, searching endlessly for someone wonderful to step out of the darkness and change my life. It never crossed my mind that that person could be me.* "
>
> —ANNA QUINDLEN,
> *New York Times* columnist,
> Pulitzer Prize winner and author of *A Short Guide to a Happy Life*

PART 2

BRAND YOU DEFINED

> *Inside of you lies all the talents you'll ever need to be amazingly successful.*
>
> **ROBIN RYAN**

CHAPTER 3

DEFINE YOUR CAREER IDENTITY

o matter how incredibly great you are at something, if others don't recognize your strengths and talents, your career will go nowhere. The most common tool we use to represent our brand is a resumé. It takes time, effort, and self-analysis to concisely articulate who you are and what you've done, leading to the promise of what you can do for an employer. Entire books (including one of mine) are devoted to teaching how to write a terrific resumé. For our purpose, it's imperative that you plainly and clearly define *Brand You* in your resumé. Your strengths must be apparent and the results you achieved using those strengths have to be noted. This is a key persuasive tool, particularly when looking for a new position or trying to land a promotion.

Another tool you can use to define *Brand You* is a brief written paragraph summarizing your brand. If nothing else, it helps you quickly clarify in your own mind what you have to offer, and if used correctly, this summary can also be very useful during interviews or when networking. But putting it together is much easier said than done. It requires you to be both clear and concise. You must be thorough in your self-analysis. As you go through the upcoming chapters, you'll have the chance to write this career identity summary.

There is one other tool that some of my clients find useful, enabling them to "see" their strengths. This tool is called a mind map, which is a visual chart that illustrates an individual's special talents and strengths.

Tony Buzan, author of *The Mind Map Book,* defines a mind map as the ultimate organizational thinking tool. A mind map allows your creativity to flow—"to think as you were designed to think," Buzan states—using two main things the brain employs during learning: association and imagination. "This thinking tool is effective because it is based on the way the brain really works," notes Buzan.

I was first introduced to mind maps years ago when Tony Buzan shared his cutting edge research at a university seminar. Today it is a popular tool used by speakers, authors, creative types, and leaders. The charts are fun to make, often drawn in color, with a center core and numerous branches to illustrate strengths and talent. I sometimes use these mind maps with my clients to help them illustrate their personal brands.

Here is an example of a mind map. This was created for the eBay project manager mentioned in chapter two.

His mind map helped him articulate that he was a proven leader with solid project management skills. He was a terrific problem solver with excellent analytical, organizational, developmental, and strategic planning abilities. He was recognized

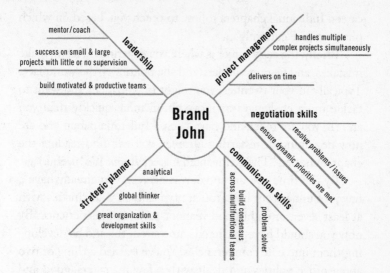

for his strong interpersonal communication and negotiation skills; his leadership ability; his effectiveness in building consensus; and his proven track record for meeting goals and deadlines. He was known for introducing innovative and creative solutions to solve problems, and excelled in mentoring team members and in building productive relationships with everyone he encountered.

Mind maps are easy to do. You only need a sheet of blank paper, colored pens or markers, and your defined strengths, with a bit of imagination thrown in. There are a few mind map examples included, along with some clients' stories, in the pages that follow.

Do use this mind-mapping tool to define *Brand You* if it is helpful. It is an easy way to lay it all out. You'll find more examples of mind mapping on www.Soaringon.com.

To properly define *Brand You*, though, you need to recognize what phase of your career you are in. There are four stages that employees typically experience over a working lifetime. They are early career, midcareer, executive career, and reinvented career. Individual chapters follow to coach you, based on which phase you are currently in.

Briefly, the early career is where you experiment, learn, make mistakes, and begin to understand the politics of the workplace. Typically in your twenties, you might be impatient and want to tackle more challenges or move ahead more quickly than you are. (If you are older, and have been a full-time parent and are now beginning or restarting a career, you will find reading the chapter entitled "The Reinvented Career *Brand You*" useful.)

By the time you are in your midcareer, you already have a few jobs under your belt. You are typically in your thirties with at least seven or eight good years of solid work experience. By now you should have mastered some strengths and be developing them into core competencies. You've learned a thing or two about office politics and dealt with a few managers, good and bad. In other words, you know the ropes. Midcareer is decision making time. You realize what kinds of sacrifices are involved in achieving major top-level VP, CEO, executive director, or general manager positions. Relocations, stress, and long work hours come with the territory when you're moving up. By age forty, typically you're married and may have children, and that greatly impacts your midcareer decisions. Some decide that they want to plateau their careers; that the sacrifices aren't worth the efforts required to move higher up the corporate ladder. Women (and some dads) may take extensive time off to care for their children.

A reality of midcareer is the realization that your career is no longer a separate issue, but an integrated part of your whole life. The best thing about being midstream is that the entire world can still be yours. You have so many choices and potential rewards. You can be targeting a promotion, starting a business, working from home, slowing down, entering a new field, putting your career in fast-forward, redesigning the job you have, changing careers, going back to college—your future is filled with possibilities that you control.

Being in the executive career stage means you've accomplished a great deal, and have recognized strengths and evident core competencies. You are either a C-level person (CEO, CFO, CTO, COO), vice president, general manager, executive director, or partner in the firm. Your challenge is to retain career vibrancy by managing through the difficulties of corporate turnovers, mergers, acquisitions, and personality clashes. You need to be very clear on *Brand You* and your career goals. You are very well established, or should be. It is wise to be open to new opportunities, and be prepared for a layoff or termination. You have lots of choices at this stage. You can cherry-pick your job, find bigger challenges, but don't let resting on your laurels be one of the options. Your job may end abruptly, launching you into retirement sooner than you had planned.

The reinvented career is defined as the stage when a person is either changing careers, reentering the workplace, or has been a long-term, undernoticed employee. The major career emphasis is on change—changing the work, the tasks, the position, or the company. Solid planning is essential to successfully navigate these waters.

It is common for people who are reinventing themselves for a major career change to seek career counseling or human resource guidance to identify their strengths. They are often confused and feel adrift or are a bit lost, wondering what to do next. If you've been regularly employed, you may worry about needing to take a reduction in salary to make a change.

Take time to be clear on your values, to assess your passion, and to focus on targeted and achievable goals. People at this stage often return to college and get a new degree or take specialized training. For example, more people in their late thirties and forties are entering law schools and MBA programs to refocus their career. New training is often essential to a major change in career direction.

In summary, *Brand You* is best defined in written form. It must include your targeted resumé, and a clear statement or mind map. This can and should be done in whatever phase of your career you are in—early, mid, executive, or reinvented. There are appropriate steps for advancing at every stage.

In the chapters that follow, *Brand You* is detailed for the stages we've defined above. Since your career needs vary as you progress along a career path, you can skip the chapters dealing with the other stages and go right to the appropriate stage for you. This will help fast-forward the defining *Brand You* process.

> *You have brains in your head. You have feet in your shoes. You can steer yourself any direction you choose.*
>
> **DR. SEUSS,**
> author of children's books

CHAPTER 4

THE EARLY CAREER
BRAND YOU

You're ready to launch or jump-start your career. You may have recently graduated from college, having invested thousands of dollars for that coveted diploma and you want it to pay off. At this stage, several important questions stare you in the face: What will you do? Where will you work? When will you get promoted? How much money will you make? Many people feel lost when they consider the endless list of career choices and fields they could go into. Add to that the list of so many potential employers and it's easy to see why one can get overwhelmed. It's a confusing and sometimes frustrating time.

You may try out one career or company and dislike it. You may be very lucky and quickly fall into something you do enjoy. Instead of drifting with the fates, it's wiser to have a specific plan to create your own career identify and advance it based on your natural talents and skills. You uncover who *Brand You* is and build upon it.

As a career counselor it's pretty common for me to see people eager to get their careers moving, but they do not know how. I've seen a few errors made repeatedly. Dave, who loved sports and had played baseball throughout his college years, had his heart set on working for Nike. He had never clearly defined, even in his own mind, what kind of job he could do for Nike. When a family friend arranged for a meeting with someone at Nike, Dave naively hoped the man would find him a job within the company. Dave never stated what he could do, or how he might best fit in at Nike, so nothing ever happened after that meeting. It wasn't the Nike employee's job to figure out what career Dave could do—it was Dave's responsibility.

Then there was Allison, a history major who expected to work as an event planner but, unfortunately, no one had hired her. She'd sent out hundreds of resumés but got no interviews. When she called employers, everyone said the same thing—*we need experience*. She was frustrated and didn't understand what she was doing wrong.

Elena went to college at twenty-five after a few years at home with her children. She majored in psychology and thought she might want a counselor job. A friend's mom who worked in human resources pointed out that Elena's verbal skills were pretty weak and that was a necessary counseling skill. Elena recognized this to be true, and felt even more lost as to what direction to pursue.

Each one of these individuals suffered from not doing some solid career exploration first. They should have assessed their strengths and done some research to get a clear idea of the types of jobs they could do using those strengths. For example, during Dave's counseling session, we looked at his strengths and had him focus on his stronger skills—editing and computer expertise. He started networking with college alumni with the specific goal of seeking a communications position. He landed a job as an editorial assistant at a company that published comic books and that was coming out with a new baseball video game. The key lesson learned was that Dave needed to focus on what he could do for an employer instead of what an employer could do for him.

Allison had sent out hundreds of resumés but got no interviews. We trimmed her two-page resumé to one page, took out the excess phrases, introduced action verbs—such as directed, organized, planned—and illustrated her accomplishments, strengths, and strongest skills. I also suggested that she volunteer to work as an intern for six weeks to learn about the meeting planning business and get some experience for the resumé. She did, and within three weeks, Allison got a job offer after she followed up on a lead from someone in the office she interned at. When her internship supervisor got called for a reference, he offered Allison a paid position with his company.

Elena had excelled in her only job before having her kids, working at a pizza place. She was organized, courteous to customers, and efficient. Her productivity led to an assistant manager's job, where she improved sales by suggesting optional items to customers and ensuring speedy delivery. We explored store management as a career. Her organizational skills and ability to think like her customers landed her a deli manager position for a large grocery store. It launched her new career and she's done very well since then.

As you are about to define your own career identify, keep in mind that you may begin to display some talents you didn't recognize you had. That's the exciting part of this career stage—

exploring, trying things out, learning, improving, and achieving success. You can make educated career choices by:

- identifying the job you want to do
- conducting research to learn the actual job duties
- interviewing people performing the job to separate your fantasy from the daily reality of the work

Launching a career is exciting, but it's also filled with potholes, valleys, troughs, detours, and an occasional disaster. You will make mistakes, get burned a few times, and realize that some coworkers are quite manipulative, problematic, and difficult. Office politics, you'll find, can be downright mindboggling. You'll benefit from developing a friend or two and a mentor to help you learn the ropes.

With about eleven thousand workdays ahead of you, focus on creating a rewarding life. Be picky about the position you do select. Your goal at this early career stage should be getting good, solid experience. Select a position in which you will learn a great deal from your new boss. Seek a manager who appears to take an interest in you and your professional development. His or her mentorship and guidance will set the stage for fast future job growth, so choose carefully. As you investigate potential employers consider all the possibilities. The *Fortune* 500, and the magnet companies (the ones *everybody* wants to work for) have fierce competition for any opening. Their websites attract two thousand to three thousand resumés *each day*. If you do get hired, you'll find a bureaucracy of policies, procedures, and rules to follow. You'll likely have a small segment of a job with little to no responsibility. You will enjoy a nice salary and benefits, but promotions may be harder to come by.

Faster professional growth typically comes by spending your first few years working for small companies (fewer than one hundred employees). Midsize organizations (fewer than five thousand employees) can be a good avenue, too. The key benefit is that in smaller offices you'll quickly get more responsibility and that will help propel your career along into future jobs. An often overlooked area is the nonprofit and government sectors. These places offer many career options, so include them in your research to determine where to go for your next job.

At your current organization be sure to work closely with HR and your boss to stay on top of any training needed to qualify for internal opportunities as they become available. Establish *Brand You* and network! It's your best weapon for gathering inside information, becoming more visible, and getting promoted.

As you start off your career, invest the time to cultivate solid relationships. Ideally your boss is the best person to try to cultivate as a mentor, but another manager might also be beneficial. You need an older, wiser confidant to help you handle coworkers or deal with office politics. Situational politics can ruin your career, so you want to get a "heads up" to avoid snafus, suicidal career errors, or glaring mistakes. Don't think people with titles hold all the power. More often people with key roles such as executive assistants know more about who is doing what and what is going on than bosses do. Make an effort to learn the lay of the land wherever you are employed.

To further fast-forward your career, join a professional association for your field. For example, accountants can join their state's CPA society, or those in HR, the local Society for Human Resource Management chapter, and lawyers, the bar association. These professional groups and associations will allow you to expand your technical skills and your network by learning from those who excel in your new field.

Careers are built one step at a time. At this early stage, employers are looking to evaluate your potential. Today employers expect you to deliver on what you promise. If you say you are great at creating Excel spreadsheets, you had better be. They want you to be reliable and flexible—willing to learn new things, to grow, and to develop, as well as get along with the rest of the work team.

UNDERSTANDING YOUR UNIQUENESS

WHEN STARTING OUT on your early career, you need to clearly review what makes you a standout person. What are the key talents and traits that make you YOU. It's critically important to do a thorough self-analysis to determine exactly what your top strengths are, define *Brand You*, and look for opportunities where those are indeed the skills the organization wants and needs.

Eventually, we're going to compile all the self-assessment materials that you completed in chapter two to define *Brand You*, but before you begin your own process, let's first look at two clients and how this process worked in their situations so you'll have good examples to follow.

James and Jennifer are appropriate case studies to best illustrate the way to define early career *Brand You*. Both had some natural teaching talent, but each used his or her talents in a personal and unique way.

JAMES—Looking for Direction

Born and raised in Puerto Rico, James met an American student while visiting Florida and eventually moved to the United States. He got married and settled in North Carolina when his new wife received a promotion there.

He had no stateside work experience and had moved to a

small town where job opportunities were few and far between. As he began to launch his career, he quickly felt overwhelmed, lost, and was without direction. Recognizing that he would need help, he began coaching sessions to get solid job search guidance. To begin, I suggested he take a step back and analyze his talents and past skills.

STEP 1: Your Brand Equity

Identify your key talents.

James had acquired some technology skills and showed his natural strengths by helping others to utilize the computer. He had a knack for languages, easily switching from Spanish to English, so he had worked in the computer lab helping other students in both languages. Additionally, James had done some nonpaid work as a tutor and had gained some experience as a teaching assistant for one of his professors.

Here are the key strengths we identified:

- customer service
- tutoring others
- instructing others in computer technology
- creating course outlines
- creativity in developing PowerPoint presentations
- administration and record keeping
- fluent language skills in both English and Spanish

STEP 2: Your Brand Advantage

Define your core competency work strengths.

James had overlooked an important area of previous experience—his volunteer work. He thought only paid employment counted. He was incorrect in that assumption.

Looking at his skills and experience we determined his core competencies to be:

- teaching others computer skills
- bilingual
- customer service

List no less than three work accomplishments that you are proud of.

1. Developed two new training courses for new and intermediate computer users.
2. Created PowerPoint presentations for class curriculum.
3. Developed lesson plans and hands-on exercises.

List education, degrees, and special training you have.

Bachelor's Degree, University of Puerto Rico

STEP 3: Your Brand Passion and Brand Values

Define your greatest interests and values.

Note: These typically need to be combined, since passion, such as teaching, and values, such as helping others, are the foundation when making choices about your career.

James felt that since teaching others was so easy and enjoyable for him, he should pursue a career in education. He valued being bilingual and felt helping others was a true calling. This decision meant he'd need to get a teaching certificate, so he'd have to return to college now that he was residing in the United States.

STEP 4: Your Brand Essence

Define your personality traits.

- friendly and nice
- helpful
- enjoys people
- curious
- loves learning
- more introverted than extroverted
- likes to be well organized and plan things
- neat

STEP 5: Your Brand Image

Define your professional image and outward appearance.

James's image needed a serious overhaul. He was exceptionally good looking, but his very sexy persona would be out of line for the work world. He did not own a suit and his interview clothes seemed more appropriate for the dance floor than job interviews. James had very little money, so his mom pitched in and bought him a nice suit. He cut his hair in a more contemporary, conservative style, and worked on presenting himself in a more professional way. He dramatically toned down the Latin lover image, and worked hard to eliminate slang phrases from his vocabulary.

STEP 6: Your Brand Workplace

Define kind of workplace where Brand You *can flourish.*

This is an important element many people forget to consider. Everyone needs a workplace where *Brand You* is nurtured and where there's an opportunity to productively apply yourself. While some people thrive in a large corporation, others might need an entrepreneurial business environment to do well. One person may be bored unless there are fast-paced challenges, and a different soul may work best in a casual, no pressure world. Different people definitely work better in certain settings. Note the workplace environment and culture you think you perform at your best in.

James realized that he wanted to work at a university, college, or school that was internationally diverse, that encouraged learning, and allowed him autonomy to do his job.

LAST STEP

Write out a brief and concise Brand You *linking all steps above.*

James wrote his example.

> I am bilingual and bicultural and I have always found languages easy to learn and use. It's my love of learning and serving others combined with my computer strengths and creative ability to teach lessons and classes so others can comprehend and apply the skills taught that I most enjoy. Being a teacher in an international program seems an ideal fit.

JAMES'S RESUMÉ

The rewriting of his resumé was a most eye-opening experience because James had dismissed or devalued what came to him so naturally. Once he knew his strengths, we reviewed all his work experience to create this winning resumé.

James Hernandez

P.O. Box 172 • Henderson, NC 21311
828-555-1212 ◆ jameshern@hotmail.com

Career Objective: Instructional or Technology Technician and/or Teaching Assistant

Summary of Qualifications

Proven experience in training, technology, and as an instructional assistant, having taught computer and software usage courses. Served as tutor for college students for Spanish/ESL programs. Strengths include: technology skills, customer service, research, instructional assistance. Bilingual and bicultural in Spanish and English.

Professional Experience

Teaching Experience

- Provided instructional assistance to teachers and students in three summer school programs. Responsibilities included: grading; preparing course materials; setting up technology and audiovisual equipment; supervising classroom; proctoring exams.
- Developed two new computer training programs for beginner and intermediate level users. Added visual components to improve the learning process using PowerPoint illustrations, created lesson plans to meet the audience needs and learning level objectives, improving the hands-on experience.
- Taught several employee training classes on customer service, computer usage, and system troubleshooting.
- Tutored college students in upper level courses in psychology, English, and Spanish.
- Created numerous PowerPoint presentations used in instructional and sales presentations.

- Worked as research lab assistant for national health research handling test samples.

Computer

- Redesigned and maintained the website for two companies handling design and programming.
- Conducted software testing on a custom-made payment system for a government project.
- Developed curriculum and computer course preparation and training.
- Conducted statistical surveys and data collection, developed questionnaires, and interviewed study participants.
- Prepared PowerPoint presentations that led to sales and better understanding of our competitiveness in the marketplace.
- Coedited the company's newsletter, which increased communication and company unity.
- Supervised and designed reports and logs in Excel to measure productivity.

Work History

- *Marketing and Web Coordinator,* DIRECTV, Carolina, PR, 2001–3
- *Trainer/Marketing Representative*, Computer Solutions of PR, Bayamón, PR, 1999–2001
- *Teaching Assistant,* Oviedo High School
- *Tutor,* College of Notre Dame Puerto Rico, 1996–1997

Education

Bachelor's Degree, Psychology, University of Puerto Rico, 2004

What Happened to James?

He landed a position as an international customer service representative in a help desk area using both English and Spanish to answer computer questions while he pursed his teaching certificate courses at night.

JENNIFER—Hoping to Move Up

Jennifer was promoted to supervisor in the customer service area for her only employer, AT&T, where she'd been working for four years. Her dream and ultimate goal was to be a corporate trainer. She had taken some classes on public speaking and she had even volunteered and taught orientation for the new employees in her department, but she had no formal teaching experience. She found she had a true passion for teaching adults how to improve on the job.

When AT&T had a full-time opening for a trainer, Jennifer wanted to apply. She came to me to help her become more competitive and land this job. She knew the competition would be keen since the job was open to internal and outside applicants and she did not have a four-year degree. More than four hundred qualified applicants applied.

STEP 1: Your Brand Equity

Identify your key talents.

To begin, we looked at her strengths. She had natural talent but little actual classroom training experience. We decided these were her key areas of strengths and talents:

- five years of customer service experience inside AT&T
- supervised AT&T employees in customer service and sales
- great communicator
- good at developing PowerPoint presentations and training materials
- trained all new employees in her department
- good problem solver

STEP 2: Your Brand Advantage

Define your core competency work strengths.

- supervised AT&T employees in customer service and sales
- great communicator

List no less than three work accomplishments that you are proud of.

- Developed a training manual for new hires on basic customer service procedures.
- Supervised employees on sales and customer service techniques.
- Created numerous employee PowerPoint presentations.
- Improved service satisfaction levels from 67% to 81% by teaching reps new and effective service strategies and also providing them with written solutions to common problems.

List education, degrees, and special training you have.

No university experience

STEP 3: Your Brand Passion and Brand Values

Jennifer loved teaching others and realized she had a natural ability to do so.

STEP 4: Your Brand Essence

Define your personality traits.

- warm
- personable
- service orientated
- likeable—easily makes friends
- interest in others
- helpful
- enjoys people
- funny

STEP 5: Your Brand Image

Define your professional image and outward appearance.

Jennifer was a very sweet, friendly person and had a pleasant speaking voice. That's a key asset in handling telephone customer service. Her image was professional, casual, and youthful for the AT&T workplace, and her attire consisted of dress pants and nice blouses with the occasional blazer and skirt. Wanting to be seen as a manager and an upwardly mobile professional, she had a nice suit for interviews. Her hairstyle, though, made her look like she was sixteen years old. Overbleached, brittle, and frizzy, her hair was in need of a new style that left the college look behind. She went to a recommended stylist who returned her hair to its natural light brown color and gave her a more classic, sophisticated cut. One more change she made for the interview was to wear only one earring in each ear (normally she wore two or three).

STEP 6: Your Brand Workplace

Define the workplace environment where you flourish and are most productive.

Jennifer liked AT&T, did very well there, and wanted to stay with the company.

LAST STEP

Write out a brief and concise Brand You *concisely linking all steps above OR create a mind map.*

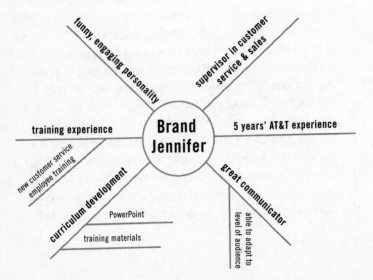

What Happened to Jennifer?

Her internal reputation, career identity, and perceived potential, plus her new resumé and the interview preparation all paid off. Jennifer got the promotion and secured a $10,000 salary increase in her new position as corporate trainer.

So now that we've taken a look at a couple of strong examples of how *Brand You* has helped two people succeed in their early career lives, turn to page 141 to create your own personal *Brand You*.

> *How do you go from where you are to where you want to be? You must have enthusiasm for life, you must have a dream or goal, and you must be willing to work for it.*
>
> **ROBIN RYAN**

CHAPTER 5

THE MIDCAREER
BRAND YOU

re you on track? Are you where you want to be? Bored? Dissatisfied? Need more challenges? Are you eyeing a promotion? A more flexible position? A new job? Just want to be better recognized? Are you unemployed and need a new start?

By midcareer, you know the lay of the land. You're in your middle to late thirties or forties, and you have probably completed college or professional studies. You have been working for several years now and have acquired some expertise. You are able to deliver specific results and possess core competencies.

At this point, your big motivations come from wanting something more or different, and/or wanting a salary increase. You need to consider if you are using your talents and strengths daily. Ask yourself: am I passionate about my work and the field I'm working in? If the answer is no, why haven't you moved on to something that can make you happier?

Midcareer isn't only about promotions, fame, and glory. It's at this stage that life, with both good and bad events, impacts on your desires, dreams, and determination. The rose-colored glasses or Pollyanna approach to your career fades as a truer reality sets in.

You've seen what a rising career demands. Sacrifice, long hours, and often a lot of travel. You may be married, have children, or be thinking about starting a family. Most women find that babies and toddlers usually slow down and plateau their professional life. Careers can and often do restart, but there is a definite "time out" period with infants at home. That's okay if you are well established but that isn't always the case. And as a working mom, you need to be careful to preserve your career reputation by remaining productive and dependable in the office. It's not an easy role for any working parent to pull off. Decisions to seek promotions are weighed against time demands away from the family, since more responsibility often mandates more hours at work.

At this career stage, men are often focused on driving hard for success. Most continue advancing their careers after children come along, working longer hours in an effort to move up, earn a better salary and be rewarded for their efforts. Throw some regular business travel into the more demanding mix, and it can be difficult to carve out family time. And even when you get a semiregular schedule, promotions often require relocating, and that just shakes everything up.

These are the hard push years for anyone eyeing upward mobility. At this stage, you should have documented accomplishments, identified core competencies, and been recognized for your strengths. Your focus is on achieving success and delivering results. You should now be much more specific in defining what you do and don't want from your career. It's also the time when you are more aware of competition as the promotion opportunities are fewer, and more people are vying for them.

This is also the point at which you start hitting your peak earning years as you live through your forties. Your salary has grown, but at some point you realize you are underpaid—that's the motivation that brings a great many clients to my business. They want to move up financially. You need to take stock of what your skills are worth. Determine if you are being underpaid. Visit www.RobinRyan.com and under tools use the salary tools to determine your true marketplace value.

Some people become too comfortable in their niches. They reach a stage where they are tempted to rest on their laurels. That's a key mistake. If you become complacent, you endanger your future and may find yourself in the unemployment line, blindsided by a layoff. You need to be prepared to meet opportunity (such as a promotion) and any adversity. Layoffs are a minefield in any position at every organization and occur when you least expect them or are ill prepared to handle them.

Brand You is most critical at this time, shaping the direction of your future. *Brand You*, when effectively established, will begin to deliver the flexibility, the positions, and the salary you want. And being recognized as a standout for your talents is essential to recession proofing your career.

Brand You comes into play for getting the most out of your internal and external networks. You must routinely invest the time to cultivate professional relationships, big and small, and see that *Brand You* is visible to others.

John, a former client, was an engineer from Austin who had a very progressive career in technical sales. He was promoted quickly several times. The last position moved him to the sales area of the company as the technical sales consulting engineer. It was a good job with a nice salary, but the position demanded tremendous amounts of travel. After his company went through a merger, he was forced to relocate to a small town in Ohio. His wife and children hated the area. They longed for their friends and the warm southern climate they'd left behind. After several months the family was absolutely miserable. John's wife moved back to Austin and got her old job back. John, faced with this family crisis, asked for a transfer but the company refused his request. He decided to quit and followed his family back to Texas. As we discussed his situation in counseling sessions, John gained some insight. First and foremost, he examined his strengths, track record, and achievements. *Brand John* was well developed and he felt he could, indeed, be selective about future positions and where they were located. Within a few months, he had networked successfully and a former boss referred him to a contact who hired him for what turned out to be a great technical sales job, making $20,000 more in base salary than at the one he had quit. *Brand John* shined through and, as he said, "saved the day."

John's former colleagues, clients, and bosses were the power in his network. He had a reputation for combining his good interpersonal skills with his technical engineering knowledge. It was an old boss who recommended him to the new company and that reference held powerful weight.

Visible accomplishments such as community service, association work, or awards you have acquired all add up to your reputation, or how the outside world sees you. Endeavor to foster your career identity as it aids you in all levels of your work and future.

Just as John had a rough ride after his company's merger, you may face a changing marketplace where your old skills must be replaced or updated. You need to continually invest in improving your skillset. Always keep learning, continually strive to expand, improve, and adapt.

Defining *Brand You* requires an investigation into all your former experience, plus any clubs or activities you're part of and community service, temporary, or volunteer work you've done. You must consider what exactly your top strengths are and understand how you have applied those gifts. Employers are looking at you to evaluate your future potential based on your past performance. They want you to be reliable and flexible—willing to learn new things, to grow and develop as well as get along with the rest of the work team. Most of all, employers expect you to deliver on what you promise and get results. If you say you are great at reorganizing office processes, you had better be. Additionally, a little soul searching is important to ensure your work is meaningful and satisfying to you.

UNDERSTANDING YOUR UNIQUENESS

YOU NEED TO clearly review what makes you a standout person. What are the key talents and traits that make you YOU. It's critically important to do a thorough self-analysis to determine exactly what your top strengths are, define *Brand You*, and look for opportunities where those are indeed the skills that the organization wants and needs.

We're going to compile all the self-assessment materials that you've completed in chapter two to define *Brand You*, but before you begin your process, let's first look at two clients and how this process worked in their situations so you'll have good examples to follow.

CARL—Handling a Layoff

arl was devastated when he lost his dream job. For thirteen years, he was the wine purchaser for a distribution company, until a bigger firm bought it out and he was out of a job. Scared and worried, he said, "Who will hire me? Where can I go? I'm fifty and all I know is wine. I'll never find anything half as good as what I lost." His fear wasn't unwarranted. The wine industry is small and his type of job was rare. Also, Carl's self-esteem was in tatters after the layoff and he seemed a little lost, leaving part of his identity behind when he was let go. Being unsure of where he'd find a new job had put him into a negative tailspin. He had no network to speak of and no resumé prepared and was terrified that his career was ruined, but he still needed to work. Identifying his personal brand got him back on track.

STEP 1: Your Brand Equity

Identify your key talents.

His first task was to evaluate his strengths.
Here are the key strengths we identified:

- deal making
- customer service
- resourceful problem solver
- negotiation skills
- great tracking, follow-up, and organizational skills
- extensive knowledge about wines

STEP 2: Your Brand Advantage

Define your core competency work strengths.

- buying wines
- deal making and negotiations
- customer service
- resourcefulness

List no less than three work accomplishments that you are most proud of.

- Have thirteen years of purchasing experience buying 61% of the entire company's sellable goods.
- Developed a network of distributors to source and purchase products to meet special customers' needs to maximize service and profits.
- Negotiated hundreds of contracts securing better terms, freight charges, and shipping fees.
- Created new computerized inventory tracking system with sophisticated forecasting function to track sales and project future trends.

List education, degrees, and special training you have.

Bachelor's Degree, Redlands University

STEP 3: Your Brand Passion and Brand Values

Wine! Not much else mattered. Corporate stability and autonomy on the job were the key traits he looked for in a new company.

STEP 4: Your Brand Essence

Describe your personality.

- good phone voice
- resourceful
- persuasive
- service oriented
- thorough—a detail person
- introverted but friendly
- well organized
- analytical

STEP 5: Your Brand Image

Define your professional image and outward appearance.

Carl noted that when you work in the purchasing department few people ever see you. His image was causal—Dockers pants and polo shirts. Contemporary but conservative. He did own a few suits and wore them when he needed to meet with special clients or attend corporate events.

STEP 6: Your Brand Reputation

Describe other people's perceptions of you.

Carl's old boss had given him complete autonomy over wine purchasing decisions, saying, "You know how to do this better than anyone else."

STEP 7: Your Brand Workplace

Define the workplace environment where you flourish and are most productive.

Large wine distribution company.

LAST STEP

Write out a brief Brand You *concisely linking all steps above or create a mind map or a strong resumé.*

In Carl's case we created a very strong resumé that outlined his key strengths, talents, and accomplishments. In creating his resumé, we covered his key contributions and clearly used the resumé's "Summary of Qualifications" section to note his brand offerings. You can see what a transformation happened by looking at the specifics Carl had mastered and accomplished.

Carl Tenneson

623 NW 44th Street
Miami, FL 32100
(941) 555-1212
Carltenns@aol.com

CAREER OBJECTIVE: Buyer/Purchasing and/or Inventory Control Position

SUMMARY OF QUALIFICATIONS

Thirteen years of purchasing experience for beverage distributor with annual sales of more than $100 million, buying 61% of the entire company's sellable goods. Extensive experience in inventory control,

---

increasing profitability while decreasing loss from spoilage. Possess sophisticated computerized tracking skills creating new systems, forecasting models, and sales reports. Proven inside sales experience selling at wholesale level with significant up-selling record. Recognized for delivering superior service to internal and external customers.

PROFESSIONAL EXPERIENCE

Inventory Analyst, Temporary Contracts, Atlantic Food Products, Miami, Fl 2004–5
Purchasing Specialist, Imports Distributing, Coral Gables, FL 1999–2003
Sales Administrator, Napa Vineyards, Napa, CA, 1985–1990

Purchasing/Buyer and Inventory

- Thirteen years of purchasing experience for beverage distributor with annual sales of more than $100 million, buying 61% of the entire company's sellable goods. Duties included: computerized and physical inventory control; buyer of multibrands and products; coordinated logistics and distribution of date-sensitive products; and managed computerized tracking system.
- Established a new purchasing system to improve inventory control and lower amount of unsellable spoiled products. Results reduced waste to lowest in industry of less than 1%.
- Buyer of multibrands and products involving purchasing, tracking sales, computerized inventory control, documenting new business trends, adjusting for seasonal and special events planning, tracking sales, and compiling complex executive team sales reports.
- Developed a network of distributors to source and purchase products to meet special customers' needs to maximize service and profits.

- Negotiated hundreds of contracts securing better terms, freight charges, and shipping fees.
- Created new computerized inventory tracking system with sophisticated forecasting function for more than 16,000 state "lottery games" to track sales and project future trends.

<u>Sales and Customer Service</u>

- Ten years of inside sales experience carrying 250 accounts selling food products and beverages at wholesale level (manufacturer to distributor). Achieved significant up-sell averages that increased sales order by more than 20%.
- Handled customer service involving hundreds of retail sales of financial services products.

EDUCATION

B.S., Business Administration, University of Redlands, CA, 1979

What Happened to Carl?

Although his resumé and brand were strong and powerful, Carl did face a serious obstacle. He loved the wine business as a buyer, and wanted to remain in it. Yet he was the first to acknowledge that his previous job was quite rare. He found nothing in the newspaper, or on websites. But at my urging, he did network. Looking for a needle in a haystack, he found one. An acquaintance told him that Princess Cruises had a buyer opening for its beverage division, mostly purchasing wines. His resumé went in and days later he was called for an interview. He went in very well prepared, and Carl was ecstatic when he landed the job with a nice salary increase, too. He emailed me recently saying, "My job's a blast—I love it. And getting cruises as perks is very cool, too. Talk about a dream job!"

Although Carl was down right after being laid off and saw major roadblocks, it was changing his mind-set, seeing the value in his brand and utilizing his network—people familiar with his brand and accomplishments—and using his key strengths that resulted in his landing a terrific job.

TERESA—Seeking a Promotion

Teresa, a petite, stocky, and studious woman with sparkling gray blue eyes and a charming smile, had ten years experience as a project manager in the biotech industry. She had a chemistry degree, plus five years experience handling FDA and regulatory compliance with extensive coursework in that area. Her credentials were very strong. She wanted to move up but the number of senior positions in the industry are very few. To land the one she really wanted within her company she needed to establish and advertise her personal brand, a task she found challenging to do.

STEP 1: Your Brand Equity

Identify your key talents.

We spent some time identifying her strengths and the key attributes necessary for a senior project manager position. These included:

- strategic planning
- eleven year's experience in project management in a scientific environment

- strong communication skills—being especially adept at conversing with scientific colleagues and technical and nontechnical staff equally well
- extensive experience and knowledge in clinical manufacturing practices
- five years in regulatory affairs
- delivering results and excelling at getting things done

STEP 2: Your Brand Advantage

Define your core competency work strengths.

- strategic planning
- good communicator
- able to drive workflow and get cooperation from others
- assimilates a great deal of information quickly
- technical writing

List no less than three work accomplishments that you are proud of.

- Developed a training manual for new hires on regulatory service procedures.
- Supervised the approval process on clinical drug trials.
- Created sophisticated tracking system to manage projects' milestones, regulatory compliance requirements, and deadlines, plus data from multiple parties.

List education, degrees, and special training you have.

BA in chemistry

STEP 3: Your Brand Passion

Define your passion and values.

- biotech research, managing projects
- making an important scientific contribution

STEP 4: Your Brand Essence

Describe your personality.

- reserved
- studious
- charming, warm smile
- obsessed with details
- thick skinned
- well organized
- a planner

STEP 5: Your Brand Image

Define your professional image and outward appearance

Stocky and short but always dressed in a very professional style in blazers and skirts or nice suits. With a pleasing, quiet manner, she got things done. Teresa was introverted but open-minded and she could be firm if necessary.

STEP 6: Your Brand Reputation

Describe other people's perceptions of you.

Teresa's boss noted that she excelled in her understanding and assimilation of the complex regulations surrounding the scientific projects she coordinated. She could build consensus, and prod people along, keeping projects in compliance and on schedule (both major challenges of her job). She had her boss's support to try to move up.

STEP 7: Your Brand Workplace

Define the workplace environment where you flourish and are most productive.

She loved the biotech field and particularly handling her research and development projects.

LAST STEP

Write out a brief Brand You *concisely linking all steps above OR create a mind map.*

Charts and graphs were common in Teresa's work so here is *Brand Teresa*'s mind map.

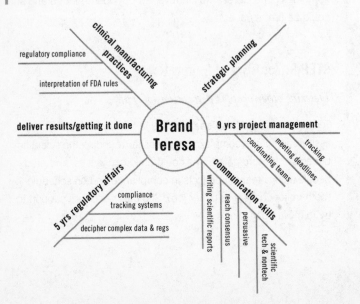

What Happened to Teresa?

She realized, once she developed her personal brand, that she could clearly illustrate strengths and core competencies to upper management in her quest for an internal promotion. She shared her goals and her map with her boss, asking for advice since the move was to another group inside the company. She interviewed with the research director for a senior level job. Although quiet and reserved, her brand stood out and today Teresa is a working at a senior level, having obtaining both her coveted promotion and a significant raise in salary.

Now that we've taken a look at how two individuals in midcareer jump-started their lives, turn to page 141 and make a plan to jump-start yours.

> *"The goal of being the very best you can be doesn't have an easy way out."*
>
> **CARLTON FISK,**
> professional baseball player

CHAPTER 6

THE EXECUTIVE CAREER
BRAND YOU

eth Godin is a worldwide best-selling author and a contributing editor to *Fast Company* magazine. In his marketing book *The Purple Cow* Godin discusses how to make a company remarkable. He uses an interesting example involving cows to make his point. He points out that after you see a few dozen black or brown and white cows, you've seen them all. They blend together—nothing special. But "What if you saw a PURPLE COW?" he questions. Now that would be something. Godin continues to use this metaphor in reviewing the plight of today's worker. Go to any big recruiting website, such as monster.com, and you'll find a database full of a million resumés, all *waiting* for someone to notice them. If your resumé is in that pile, it's not a good place to be since getting noticed is nearly impossible. Godin's book makes a key point—you need to be remarkable in what you do, then your references *become* much more important than your resumé, and you stand out as the purple cow.

Executives like yourself have already achieved a great deal of success. You have acquired good skills, molded your strengths into notable core competencies, and have a handle on what you'd like to do. But perhaps you find yourself unexpectedly looking for a new position, or wanting to move up to the next level or a larger company or take on a new or different challenges. You may seek less stress or pressure in your work life.

The competition at the top is very intense. Other executives have your skillset, and organizations are very selective these days. *Brand You* must show your distinctive uniqueness. You must get to the core of what makes you the individual you are, and be explicit about the kinds of results you can deliver. Companies today are also seeking leaders who have high ethical standards and integrity. Those are key personality traits to stress as you market yourself.

Turning yourself into a purple cow takes a great deal of time and energy, but continually building *Brand You* is something you have been doing over your lifetime. You probably wouldn't be where you are if you hadn't. Top leaders strive to become noted for their key strengths. When that happens, you are continually noticed and recommended, and as your personal brand grows, so does your title, the level of position you hold, your financial compensation, and added perks.

BEING THE NOTORIOUS PURPLE COW

CLIENTS HAVE TOLD me a story about Harry the Hatchet, an infamous executive with an appropriate nickname. He was indeed a purple cow, noted for ruthlessly cutting expenses and eliminating jobs with the stroke of his pen. This CFO had unrestricted authority to make drastic changes in order to streamline production and to reduce costs. His career identity was known throughout the company, and his reputation was frequently discussed by competitors worldwide. He had been lured away from his former employer *because* he was known as the hatchet man and had been recently asked to join a *Fortune* 100 company because of that reputation. The board of directors had been seeing a lot of red ink and they believed Harry would be an asset if he joined their team. Within eighteen months, he had turned the company's situation around—but thousands of its employees went to the unemployment lines in the process. He did indeed cut deep, resulting in greatly reduced company expenses. The bottomline began to show improvement, and Harry got the credit for returning the company to profitability. Harry the Hatchet had done what he did best. As you can imagine, he was not well liked. Never was. Never will be. Doesn't care. He's cold, steely, tough, unbending, and seemingly heartless. Nonetheless, his brand is so distinctive, he truly is a purple cow.

I don't recommend you become equally notorious. But there are a few people who have used their negative reputation and their personal *Brand You* to this end. It's who they are and why they have been successful. They meet a company's need using their strengths.

I support *Brand You* being the best you can be—whatever that is—but it is far easier for you to move ahead for positive reasons rather than negative ones.

UNDERSTANDING YOUR REMARKABILITY

YOU NEED TO clearly review what makes you a standout executive, preferably before a layoff or firing happens to you.

By the time you've reached the executive level you have a track record of accomplishments. You are likely to be in your forties or fifties, making a good salary, and have settled into a nice lifestyle. Many of you will be recruited to join a new organization and in some cases the VPs and CFOs among you will get tapped for the top job. Although you have made it, you should not let your career coast along. The fates often interfere in that nice life with an unexpected termination. Layoff. Merger. Firing. Politics. Boards wanting new blood. Whatever the reason, you may find yourself job hunting. That typically equates into at least one year of looking for another position, possible relocation, and a lot of pain and frustration along the way. No one can see into the future or prevent this fate befalling you. Even the strongest purple cow can have a skillset that's no longer needed. It's critically important to do a thorough self-analysis to determine exactly what your top strengths are, define *Brand You*, and become well known among your network. Do be on the lookout for opportunities and organizations where your leadership skills are wanted and needed.

You are about to compile all the self-assessment materials you've completed in chapter two, in order to define *Brand You*, but before you begin your own process, let's first look at two clients and how this process works so you'll have good examples to follow. The stories of Rick and Judy offer a realistic look at how two executives more clearly defined their uniqueness and how they applied their talents on the job.

RICK—Getting Back on Track

The chief of operations for a multisystem healthcare organization, Rick Arnseth had had a terrific career for more than a dozen years when he got blindsided by the company CEO and was laid off. The move devastated him. A talented man, he still needed some career counseling to bolster his self-esteem after his firing, and to get a better handle on *Brand Rick*. Although he flourished at running profitable, high-quality hospitals, he began to doubt himself because of his humiliating termination. He was not good at self-marketing. When we started working together, he described himself as a fifty-six-year-old, laid-off, depressed, fat guy. His feelings of despair are fairly typical. An executive's identity—man or woman—is typically tied up in his position, title, responsibilities, and the organization as a whole. Rick quickly grasped the need for and benefit of shaping his personal brand. A new resumé outlined his key strengths, those of being great at streamlining operations while increasing profitability and quality simultaneously. In addition, it illustrated how he excelled at building productive partnerships with physicians' groups and outside agencies. I pointed out that this layoff was the push Rick needed so he could move into the CEO role, instead of looking only at the number-two-person opportunities.

A serious makeover was needed, however. This former college athlete had a sedentary lifestyle and had grown to more than 275 pounds. At six feet, he recognized that he needed to trim the pounds that had accumulated over the years. Rick worried, and rightly so, about not being able to compete for a new job when going up against younger, healthier applicants. Long hours devoted to the career and the executive position, plus a family, had not left much time for him to take care of his physical fitness. *Fear* of not getting hired again was his motivation to undertake a strict diet and to hit the gym on a daily basis. Rick trimmed off sixty pounds in six months.

While he transformed his body, I recommended that we transform his image and personal presentation as well. A few days before he went to a big job interview Rick came to meet with me dressed in the suit that he planned to wear. Old-fashioned and drab—those were the vibes his out-of-date attire gave off, not the progressive and enthusiastic change maker his brand said he was. First to go was the greasy pomade he used on his hair. Slicked back, it made him look stern. Next, his suit was too dark a color, and when he sat down the shoulders bobbed up around his neck. It clearly did not fit him since he had lost the weight. A plain white shirt and dark tie topped off the stark, unimpressive ensemble.

Indeed the whole image was of a dated, severe, stuck-in-his-ways, cold, has-been kind of guy. This did not fit the brand that he had recently defined. Rick was innovative, a great relationship builder, terrific at managing hospital operations, friendly, approachable, and very well liked. Since he was competing for top level jobs, he needed to change his personal appearance so it was congruent with the style and brand he projected. With my shopping list in hand Rick went off to the department store. He bought a new navy blue suit that was perfectly cut for his trimmer body. He exchanged the white shirt for a pale blue one that matched the suit and bought a snazzy tie and new dress shoes to polish off the outfit. The new look gave Rick a transformed, confident air. He appeared to be the kind of executive that board members want to hire, and indeed they did!

There are many executives who unfortunately will not see that same kind of success. Rather than being recognized as standout candidates, their value will be diminished by employers. Employers and boards of directors will "see" the candidate only as "a fifty-six-year-old, laid-off, depressed, unfashionable, fat guy—or gal." Your image can project a career-killer look, saying *"dead weight,"* *"burned out,"* or *"retired on the job."* These projections can end an executive's career potential. Your image is a critical element in your brand. Review it with a discerning eye, and be sure that you look vibrant, energetic, and ready to take on the world.

STEP 1: Your Brand Equity

Identify your key talents.

Rick was blindsided by his layoff. Some politics between him and the CEO were likely behind the action, but nonetheless at fifty-six he found himself unemployed and facing the fact that the small city that he so enjoyed would need to be left behind in order to find another hospital position. His self-esteem was in tatters, and his family was greatly upset, which made him feel worse. Rick was badly in need of some esteem building—which is exactly what the *Brand You* process did for him. Since he'd been on the job for more than a dozen years, he didn't have a current resumé and the one he had created before we met was very long using an out-dated style. As we revamped his resumé, the key strengths we defined were:

- visionary leader
- cohesive team builder with physicians, hospital staff, and senior leadership
- good at streamlining operations while improving quality
- strategic planner
- able to create partnerships and alliances
- excellent at hospital development and expansion

STEP 2: Your Brand Advantage

Define your core competency work strengths.

- hospital development and expansion with visionary strategic planning

- streamlining operations while improving quality
- cohesive team builder with physicians, hospital staff, senior leadership

List no less than three work accomplishments that you are proud of.

- Achieved national recognition for hospital named in Top 100 Hospitals in the United States for four years.
- Developed new programs, including physician recruitment that has generated more than $400 million in new revenues.
- Consistently operated hospital profitably for fifteen consecutive years, while also providing superior quality patient care.
- Established six major joint ventures/partnerships that now contribute $50 million in additional revenues annually.
- Led the development, planning, construction, and operations of a new women's birthing center with neonatal and perinatal facilities.

List education, degrees, and special training you have.

Master's in Health Services Administration, University of Vermont, 1983
Bachelor's in Business Administration, University of Connecticut, 1971

STEP 3: Your Brand Passion and Brand Values

Passionate about hospital management, Rick values the ability to help others, blend work and family, operate with integrity, and have the power to initiate change.

STEP 4: Your Brand Essence

Describe your personality.

- congenial, engaging personality
- nice
- persuasive
- firm but not rigid
- planner
- social and personable
- analytical
- loves building (relationships, programs, structures)
- extroverted

STEP 5: Your Brand Image

Define your professional image and outward appearance.

Rick needed to undergo a complete makeover. He transformed himself from looking old fashioned, stern, and out-of-touch into a contemporary executive who makes things happen. In his case, the physical presentation was a radical but highly important change to support his brand. A new suit and hairstyle worked wonders.

STEP 6: Your Brand Reputation

Describe other people's perceptions of you.

Rick was a strong networker and was considered an open and honest nice guy. His congenial personality made him likeable. He had created many good relationships in the healthcare field and as a result many people offered support, introductions, inside information, and leads. His references were enthusiastic about him and his strengths. His brand had clearly been seen and respected by others.

STEP 7: Your Brand Workplace

Define the workplace environment where you flourish and are most productive.

Rick was the number two guy at his last job. I felt he was well positioned to move up into the CEO chair and advised him to look for and pursue those opportunities.

LAST STEP

Write out a brief Brand You *concisely linking all steps above or create a mind map.*

For Rick we created a sheet of his top selling points and a top-notch resumé. In his written summary he stressed the following.

A contemporary, progressive, visionary leader with demonstrated expertise in the development of an award-winning hospital, receiving a prestigious ranking in the Top 100 Hospitals in the United States for four years.

Possesses strong operations expertise; consistently operated hospital profitably for fifteen consecutive years, while also providing superior quality patient care.

Excellent strategic planner, developing new programs and adding new facilities that have generated more than $400 million in new revenues.

Most notable strengths include: strategic planning, operations management, marketing, program development, and superior skill to build a cohesive team including physicians, hospital staff, and senior leadership.

After that we spent several hours creating his new resumé. This resumé gained him an interview at every position he applied for. This is the one that captured the interest of recruiters and hiring committees.

Rick Christiano

27 Edgewater Drive
Hartford, CT 06107
860.555.7727 home • 860.555.1238 cell
Rickchri@aol.com

Career Objective: Hospital/Health System CEO or COO

SUMMARY OF QUALIFICATIONS

Visionary leader with demonstrated expertise in working successfully with physicians, provider groups, and patients to develop an award-winning hospital, receiving a prestigious ranking in the Top 100 Hospitals in the United States for four years. Possesses solid history of developing new programs, including physician recruitment that has generated more than $400 million in new revenues. Consistently operated hospital profitably for fifteen consecutive years, while also providing superior quality patient care. Notable strengths include: financial management, strategic planning, operations management, marketing, program development, and superior skills to build a cohesive team including physicians, hospital staff, and senior leadership.

PROFESSIONAL EXPERIENCE

Chief operating officer (promoted from president, executive VP)
Saint Francis Hospital and Medical Center, Hartford, CT 1988–2004

Hospital Administration

- Managed the day-to-day operations of regional tertiary hospital with rehab institute and skilled nursing facility totaling 612 beds; named one of Top 100 Hospitals in America for four years, annual revenues $410 million; 2,300 employees. Reported to the CEO of system.
- Responsibilities for daily hospital operations included: strategic planning; quality of care; financial/budget management; program development; joint ventures (physician groups/other hospitals/outside providers); staffing; physician recruitment; third-party negotiations; resource allocation; planning/development/construction of new buildings/programs; compliance and governmental regulations; overseeing services delivery.
- Created new physician recruitment program (1997) designed to attract top physicians into various groups. Program has generated a total of $245 million in new revenue, which has increased each year, to the high in 2002 of $50 million for that year.
- Established a new $57-million nationally recognized community joint venture company with competitor, to merge together and turn around business losses. New organization has 850 employees, provides air ambulance transport (fifth largest in United States); new rehabilitation institute level II joint trauma system, thirty-two-hospital information network; fundraising. Results achieved profitability in three years, plus decreased operating costs for both organizations, saving $98 million from annual operations.
- Established six major joint ventures/partnerships to incorporate orthopedics, oncology, cardiology, urology, ambulatory surgery, and cardiac surgery into the hospital structure. These partnerships now contribute $50 million in additional revenues annually.
- Led the development, planning, construction, and operations of a new women's birthing center with neonatal and perinatal facilities that increased market share from 29% to 58% and generated more than $20 million in additional annual revenues.
- Developed a new partnership with one of the country's largest

multispecialty clinics, creating the largest cancer center in the region. Results will add $30 million in new revenue this year.
- Headed the team to create a new ten-story medical building on hospital campus. Oversaw planning, design, construction, tenant recruitment, and contract negotiations. Project completed on time and on budget in 2003.

Previous Work History

Executive VP/hospital administrator (reporting to health system CEO), Eastern New Hampshire Medical Center and six affiliated hospitals, 1984–88
Assistant hospital administrator, University of Vermont Medical Center, 1981–84

AWARDS

Top 100 Hospitals in the United States—1991, 1996, 1997, 2004

EDUCATION

Master's in Health Services Administration, University of Vermont, 1983
Bachelor's in Business Administration, University of Connecticut, 1971

What Happened to Rick?

He had several interviews for CEO possibilities brewing when he landed a true dream job—CEO for a healthcare hospital system in a beautiful region of the country, with a $50,000 salary increase and attractive benefits and extra perks. *Brand Rick* had shone through once he matched his talents and reputation to his image.

JUDITH—Moving On to Bigger and Better Things

Most executives are not in transition when a company comes recruiting. Judith was doing well as CFO of a large company with $85 million in annual revenues. One day John, the CEO of a major nationally recognized company, called her. He'd gotten her name from an accountant who'd worked as an employee for her, and the accountant, aware of her brand strength, thought she'd be ideal for the position the CEO had available.

John was looking to hire a VP of finance and wanted to discuss the position with Judith. After a lengthy conversation, she and I updated her resumé and she emailed it to him. Her brand was clear: she had the necessary financial expertise and a reputation for being upright and honest, and she also possessed superior negotiation and cost-cutting skills. A master at relationships she had made good alliances with major retailers, saving her company millions in purchasing transactions. Judith's brand was well defined on her resumé, but it was the young accountant who had been an employee who sold the CEO on her strengths. That CEO needed a strong leader who had an impeccable reputation for integrity. The board of directors felt that all the new legislation and high-level scrutiny on finance operations necessitated selecting someone with a sterling reputation for honesty. Additionally, they knew that the person had to excel in motivating a team as well as being a great finance person.

Judith was as honest and ethical as they come. Those ethics had even cost her a prior job. But this CEO was drawn to that reputation and to her management skills. She had a track record of career successes at building highly productive teams with little attrition. All together, *Brand Judith* was irresistible and got a great job offer when she had not even been looking. This opportunity found her because *Brand Judith* was well established.

Incidentally, the company made her a compensation offer so lucrative that it was impossible to refuse. She's continued to be a big success—a win-win for both her and her new employer.

STEP 1: Your Brand Equity

Identify your key talents.

The CEO was interested in Judith before he had even called her after getting a stellar recommendation from her former team member, the accountant who now worked for him. Her resume solidified his opinion. Her key strengths were defined as:

- finance background, holding MBA and CPA designations
- strategic planner
- cost-cutting skills
- integrity and indisputable ethics
- cohesive team builder
- superior negotiation record with major retailers, saving her company millions in purchasing transactions

STEP 2: Your Brand Advantage

Define your core competency work strengths.

- financial leadership strategic planning
- streamlining and cost-cutting operations
- negotiating and deal-making skills
- forecasting

List no less than three work accomplishments that you are proud of.

- Provided financial leadership for international manufacturer, increasing revenues from $150 million up to $500 million.
- Made deals and alliances with major retailers, saving sev-

eral million dollars and improving bottom line profits by 5%.
- Renegotiated or changed vendors' contracts, delivering better prices and terms, saving $250,000 annually.
- Streamlined operations and financial systems, cutting costs by $1.2 million.

List education, degrees, and special training you have.

Master's in Business Administration, University of Washington
License: CPA (Certified Public Accountant)

STEP 3: Your Brand Passion and Brand Values

Business finance; expansion through negotiations; values ethical transactions and honesty, and integrity in all contacts.

STEP 4: Your Brand Essence

Describe your personality.

- honesty
- integrity—her word is gospel
- high standards of professional ethics
- shrewd
- clever problem solver
- analytical
- quiet
- introverted

STEP 5: Your Brand Image

Define your professional image and outward appearance.

Judith is petite, thin, and in her late forties; she is always dressed very conservatively in expensive and fashionable business suits. She talks with a polished British accent.

STEP 6: Your Brand Reputation

Describe other people's perceptions of you.

She excelled at leading a team and expanding business. She was very fair and ethical and was a popular manager, evidenced by her former employee's referral of her to his CEO.

STEP 7: Your Brand Workplace

Define the workplace environment where you flourish and are most productive.

She liked an expanding international organization and challenging work environment with a great deal of autonomy.

LAST STEP

Write out a brief *Brand You* concisely linking all steps above OR create a mind map.

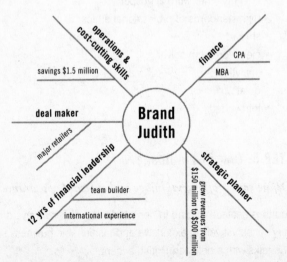

What Happened to Judith?

She had two interviews, one with the CEO and another with the board of directors, and she landed the job. The new position came with $22,000 salary increase, a much more lucrative bonus plan, stock grant, and a $20,000 signing bonus.

Now that we've taken a look at some executives who benefited from strengthening their brand, turn to page 141 and do the same for yourself.

> *Not everybody can be famous, but everybody can be great because greatness is determined by what you do.*
>
> **OPRAH WINFREY**

CHAPTER 7

THE REINVENTED CAREER
BRAND YOU

ho needs to reinvent themselves? Anyone who is changing careers or reentering the workplace or has been laid off or languishing at one company for a very long time. Sound familiar? If so, then it's time for you to do some serious career exploration, evaluate the current job market, identify your interests, and target the desired career opportunity.

Applying *Brand You* in these situations focuses heavily on using your transferable strengths, acquired from any past work, volunteer, association, or community service experiences. Transferable skills, such as planning, budgeting, organizing, scheduling, sales, or computer knowledge, are all talents you can use at one job or another. These are the key abilities that demonstrate your advanced level and desirable potential to an employer.

Talents that you've forgotten about or used a while back may resurface and play a major role in your future career endeavors. Your volunteer experience, a recent degree, a new ability you've mastered, or updates to old talents can contribute to and define the reinvented *Brand You*. You'd be surprised to learn how many people fall back on old strengths—ones they displayed in high school, college, or earlier in their careers—to redefine themselves. Here's my client Frank's revelation: "I was a good writer when I was young, but I so enjoyed making people laugh and doing comedy that I went into the entertainment field as a stand-up comic. Made a great living for a while. Then the times changed and the job opportunities dried up. I took stock of my other talents and came back to writing, but story writing wasn't my thing. I took a copywriting course and began writing funny marketing ads—it led to a whole new and prosperous career. Who'd have thought I could fall back on something I'd done so long ago."

It's important to realize that you have many talents and are multifaceted. You have been using them since childhood. You, too, can reinvent yourself and go in numerous career directions. You also possess some core competencies. You may be afraid you'll have to accept a financial back turn; be assured that this is not typically the case. When you combine your talents and transferable skills while more effectively advertising your strengths, the consolidation allows you to move on into a new field, position, or company—and to prosper!

In defining *Brand You* consider what your top strengths are and how you have applied them in the past. Take note of the results you've achieved, along with your potential, and then decide how you want to apply your gifts in your next job. But remember that as employers evaluate your future potential, they also want you to be reliable and flexible—willing to learn new things, grow, and develop—as well as get along with the rest of the work team.

Many people feel uncertain about trying to reinvent themselves. Change—any kind of change—often seems difficult. And when it comes to career changes they find excuses for not going after their dreams. I often hear people use excuses that prevent them from changing their life such as, "I'm too old to start over" or "With our bills, I can't take a pay cut." Often it's just simply self-doubt talking.

You may want to make changes, but you just don't do it. You hear the phrase you can reinvent yourself but think it's something other people accomplish, and so far you haven't made the effort. *Brand You* simply needs to be defined correctly and advertised consistently to open up a whole new world of work opportunities for you. Others have changed their lives for greater reward and prosperity, and so can you.

You may find yourself needing reinvention because of unforeseen circumstances or other dramatic life situations. Divorce, death of a parent or loved one, chronic illness, or job loss can all contribute. In those situations, change is forced upon you. Perceived obstacles such as lack of money, direction, or supportive cheerleaders may also be holding you back. You must see beyond these surmountable problems and believe in the true value that lies inside. You must acknowledge your strengths and give your talents opportunities to flourish. You have the power to make positive change. Just start by moving out of your comfort zone, no other person can do it for you. Take one step and then another, and the next ones all get much easier. Change must be generated by you. If you still remain stuck, seek professional career counseling or even psychological therapy to determine what is blocking you from greater success and a happier life.

UNDERSTANDING YOUR UNIQUENESS

THE FOLLOWING CLIENTS' examples are broken down by circumstances that likely mirror your situation. These clients' experiences are here to provide a guide that will assist you as you now customize *Brand You*.

☑ the career changer

☑ the laid-off worker

☑ the reentry job seeker

☑ the been-there-forever employee

☑ the military to civilian career switcher

JULIA—The Reinvention of a Career Changer

Sometimes life deals you a lousy hand. Julia, a tall, modellike blonde in her late thirties, faced serious obstacles to gaining employment in her chosen field. She had once had a top job in banking as a vice president of commercial lending, but then she went through a divorce, remarried, and moved to another state, leaving her successful career behind. Shortly after Julia remarried, she found out that her new husband was more than $100,000 in debt. Within a couple of months the two of them filed for bankruptcy. This action had lifetime repercussions for Julia because that bankruptcy would be a serious challenge to finding work in the financial services area again. When the marriage ended, she wanted to get back into the lucrative career she'd left behind. She needed professional help and so she became a client. At the time, she was in Orlando, selling vacation packages. Julia was the top salesperson, but the salary was around $50,000 and she wanted to return to the Northeast and again pick up her executive career, which offered the potential for significantly better compensation.

She had some good contacts and actively networked. We created a new resumé and she began to interview. Julia contacted former employees, bosses, and managers. Networking was fruitful and she had several interviews. She received a terrific job offer at a bank, but when it checked her background and discovered the bankruptcy, the offer was rescinded. The bank's policy was typical for this industry. No one with bankruptcy in their history could work in their loan office. Therefore, Julia had no choice but to leave the banking field behind.

Julia had proven strengths, however, so we used the branding process and applied it to the general area of sales. We worked on polishing her interview skills and she went out in search of employment.

STEP 1: Your Brand Equity

Identify your key talents.

- ability to create good relationships with corporate and non-profit clients
- superior customer service skills
- good problem-solving skills
- innovation in developing business
- sales abilities
- strong skills in financial analysis that allowed her to examine and identify target clients
- extraordinary perception of market research and capitalizing on trends

STEP 2: Your Brand Advantage

Define your core competency work strengths.

- improving sales production
- innovative business development leadership
- problem solving
- collaborative leadership

List no less than three work accomplishments that you are proud of.

- Ten years of top sales production and innovative business development leadership.
- Award winner
  - Chairman's Award, Outstanding Quarterly Sales, won for seven out of ten quarters
  - Recipient of Top Gun Sales Award, Marriott
- Created hundreds of sales proposals to potential associations, hospitals, and *Fortune* 500 companies.
- Handled both telemarketing and in-person sales.
- Provided sales training for both staff and management by teaching classes, leading panel discussions, and conducting sales meeting. Created sales training programs improving negotiation, sales, and service skills.

List education, degrees, and special training you have.

BS, Marketing/Management, Georgia Tech, Blacksburg, Georgia.

STEP 3: Your Brand Passion and Brand Values

Making a sale and satisfying a client, and achieving a high salary and rewards for her work were of top importance.

STEP 4: Your Brand Essence

Describe your personality.

- analytical
- persuasive
- service oriented
- creative
- problem solver
- friendly, extroverted
- charismatic
- analytical
- well liked
- terrific recall for names
- great at small talk

STEP 5: Your Brand Image

Define your professional image and outward appearance.

Julia is attractive and projects a professional demeanor, and her attire is conservative but elegant. She is very personable and able to easily make people feel comfortable talking to her.

STEP 6: Your Brand Reputation

Describe other people's perceptions of you.

Her former boss said she was a stellar employee. She had excelled at sales and customer relations and projected a great image. (He also pointed out his regret that adversity in her personal life had gotten her off track and taken her permanently out of the banking field. He cited it as a loss to them.) She relied on old connections and networking. She easily got introductions and several interviews.

STEP 7: Your Brand Workplace

Define the workplace environment where you flourish and are most productive.

A hands-off customer service environment allowing her entrepreneurial spirit to flourish.

LAST STEP

Write out a brief Brand You *concisely linking all steps above or create a mind map.*

We created a *Brand You* mind map chart as her visual tool to more clearly recognize her brand. She used it as a guide to identify her strengths and promote *Brand Julia's* best selling points as she made a necessary career change, leaving the banking world behind.

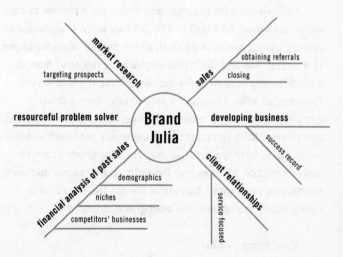

What Happened to Julia?

When you display your gifts everyone notices. Let me share with
you an e-mail that she sent me so you can see the results of the
Brand You process and how establishing her career identity
revitalized her career.

———————

To: RobinRyan@aol.com
From: Julia
Subject: I got the JOB!

    Dear Robin,
    **I'm so excited to tell you I have accepted a terrific offer with a
major publications company. I was offered a base salary of
$85,000 (I had previously earned in the banking industry a
$90,000 base after seventeen years in the business). This is terrific
since I have no experience in the publishing industry. And it's a
major step up since my Marriott position paid me about $50,000.**
    **I will also receive commissions, which are projected to earn
me an additional $30,000 to $50,000 annually. I negotiated an
upfront signing bonus of $4,000, which did not originally appear
in the offer. You and God's blessings are the reasons I have this
wonderful new beginning. By the way, during the four days
following my offer, I received a second offer from another
company, several other requests for interviews, which I declined,
and I have a third company that is extremely persistent and still
wants me to interview because they are disappointed I am no
longer available, but they love the skills on my resumé and want
to interview me anyway. Talk about the positive impact of a
strong *Brand You* resumé and selling your strengths!**

    Many thanks—Julia

———————

KATHLEEN—The Reinvention of a Career Changer with No Experience in a New Area

Kathleen loved fashion and worked at Nordstrom part-time selling men's shirts while attending college. She stayed on after graduating with a business degree and was eventually promoted to run the men's department. In her free time, she was an avid knitter and often made sweaters and vests for family and friends. Her dream was to become a knitwear designer for one of the large men's fashion houses. Living in Seattle, she nurtured the fantasy for five years, then finally felt brave enough to act upon it. She made an appointment with me to discuss the practicality of trying to completely change careers. She had no design experience and believed it to be an impossible obstacle to overcome in order to reach her dream.

Kathleen and I took stock of her strengths and skills then defined *Brand Kathleen*.

Her key talents were:

- eye for color, able to see subtle differences and nuisances
- touch sensitivity and feel for yarns
- finger dexterity
- observing nature
- finger on the pulse of purchasing habits in men's clothing
- merchandizing ability to enhance items
- sales experience selling men's clothes

In a field as closed and competitive as fashion design, I felt that only through making the right contacts would she have any chance of securing her first design job. She would need great references and fortunately she had nurtured many contacts during her Nordstrom career. She had many informational interviews but her lack of experience detoured employers from considering her for a designer position. She was discouraged but kept at it.

With the help of a distant cousin, who was connected to someone at Calvin Klein, she got an introductory interview at the company. Upon hearing about their need for project managers, Kathleen and I revamped her game plan and she stressed the organizational planning and budget management skills that illustrated the contributions she could make. Her brand demonstrated her love of learning, and the great potential and drive she brought to her job. She got her chance. Her new career was launched as a design assistant and project manager. At night she took advanced fashion design courses, continually developing her talents and skills. Kathleen worked hard and excelled when she got the chance to design. She was recently promoted to male sweater designer for the Calvin Klein label and wrote to say she had the best job in the world.

TYLER—The Reinvention of a Laid-off Worker

A tall, lean executive with a quiet, reserved attitude, Tyler had fifteen years of experience in corporate communications. It was very difficult when he got laid off from his position as an investor relations consultant (a financial PR job), since many other communications professionals also lost their jobs at the same time. Only a few positions materialized over the next several months, and the competition was intense. Being over forty compounded his fear that he would not be able to find a new position.

Tyler had trouble defining his strengths. This was ironic since he was a professional communicator. Discussing *Brand Tyler* helped him see his natural areas of ability. Specifically, we focused on his writing and editing skills, along with his project management strengths. In previous positions, he had created speeches and authored long annual reports; during his interviews, he always brought his portfolio with writing samples to show.

We identified the strengths and attributes for his brand as follows:

- fifteen years of public relations experience, including staff supervision
- writing and editing skills
- knowledgeable and experienced in creating all forms of communication: publications, correspondence, speeches, investor/financial reports, annual reports, and so on.
- project management expertise
- conservative "business suit" professional appearance

Together, we perfected his resumé and cover letter so that they strongly established his brand.

Tyler Haselman

11732-123rd Avenue SE • San Francisco, CA 94148
(415) 555-8979 • tyler.tyler21@msn.com

Washington Credit Union League
33301 9th Avenue South, Suite 200
Federal Way, WA 98003

Dear Human Resources:

Fifteen years' experience managing marketing communications and public relations, shaping positive public messages, and implementing

branding strategies is the background I'd bring to your Director of
Public Relations and Communications position.

Highlights of my background include:

- Developed and implemented communications plans for
  corporations and agencies; wrote, edited, and shaped positive
  public messages for diverse audiences.
- Produced a wide range of publications including brochures,
  articles, marketing materials, proposals, fact sheets, news releases,
  financial charts, correspondence, annual reports, newsletters, and
  PowerPoint presentations.
- Wrote speeches and phone scripts used by senior executives for
  conference calls and investor communications.
- Worked successfully with internal and external teams on project
  management.

I've worked closely with top management to develop key messages on
a company's mission, market opportunities, products, financial
picture, and strategic plan. I've handled media relations involving
writing and distributing press releases, pitching stories, and
coordinating requested interviews. I have solid expertise handling
crisis communications, managing multiple projects simultaneously,
and building highly productive teams.

I would like to discuss in greater detail the valuable contributions I
could make to your communications department. You can contact me
at (415) 555-8979.

Your time and consideration are most appreciated.

Sincerely,

Tyler Haselman

Tyler Haselman

Tyler Haselman

11732-123rd Avenue SE • San Francisco, CA 94148

(415) 555-8979 • tyler.tyler21@msn.com

CAREER OBJECTIVE: Communications Manager

SUMMARY OF QUALIFICATIONS

Recognized for outstanding communications work with fifteen years of proven expertise managing corporate communications. Strengths include: writing, editing, organization, project management, and handling media and public affairs. Well respected professional with high professional standards for achieving and exceeding goals and objectives.

PROFESSIONAL EXPERIENCE

Communications and Investor Relations Consultant, Financials.com, San Francisco, CA, 2001 to present

Vice President Finance/Director of Public Relations, John Tyler Co., Oakland, CA, 1988–2001

Assistant Professor, Mount St. Mary's College, Los Angeles, CA 1985–88

Communications/Public Relations

- Fifteen years managing corporate communications, with responsibilities including: strategic planning, creating communication plans, crisis management, media, liaison to top executives and department heads, development of corporate branding, financial communications, advertising, event planning, plus staff hiring and development.
- Wrote and edited brochures, articles, reports, correspondence; produced newsletters; created conference-call scripts, speeches, and shareholder letters for senior management; developed surveys;

contributed to annual reports; authored proposals and business plans; wrote and posted Web content.

- Analyzed new clients' goals and marketing plans to articulate corporate identity and brand for their corporate communications through marketing tools and PowerPoint presentations.
- Handled media relations involving writing and distributing press releases, pitching stories, coordinating interviews, media coaching of executives, and engaging in crisis damage control.
- Served as spokesperson/designated spokesperson to represent company.

Management

- Supervised business operations and finances, including budgets, payroll, purchasing, computer systems, and financial reporting.
- Extensive project management expertise, successfully working with internal and external teams. Established tracking and follow-up systems to meet deadlines.
- Developed highly productive teams in sync to accomplish goals and missions.
- Served in leadership roles at Kaiser and other nonprofit organizations.

COMMUNITY SERVICE HONORS

Recipient of 2001 Kaiser Health Service Award for leadership and communications work.

EDUCATION

Doctorate and master's degree, comparative literature, Syracuse University, 1985/1980
Bachelor's degree, University of California-Los Angeles, 1977

Tyler recognized that self-marketing and interviewing were areas he needed to work on so we role-played and did a few coaching sessions to help him improve his interviewing skills. He is a quiet, soft-spoken, and humble person who is not accustomed to advertising himself, but he said that the *Brand You* process was insightful and quite helpful to him. It crystallized exactly who he was and helped him articulate his strengths. It made him see that although a layoff from a large organization had hurt, and the pain of rejection was keen, he did indeed have great value.

What Happened to Tyler?

Tyler landed a terrific job as a director of communications. He was very pleased to be able to remain and thrive in a field he loves. The new job paid even more than the one he had lost, much to his amazement.

MICHAEL—The Reinvention of a Military-to-Civilian Career Switcher

Leaving behind a twenty-year officer's career in the Navy Civil Engineer Corps, Michael was surprised that the change was much more challenging than he imagined it would be. Although he'd been warned in some transition classes and by former officers that military-to-civilian job searches were difficult, he still expected it to be easy for him. After all, he had terrific communication skills and was a great networker. Nonetheless, it indeed proved to be a significant challenge. This is because Michael, like most military departees, had been living a specific way of life and was use to an assigned, *distinctive*, top-down, structured work culture. Leaving that environment meant moving completely outside a familiar comfort zone. Some people pull it off, others never get back on track, but just about every former military officer says the whole experience is a bit unnerving.

Michael was surprised to find that the business world used language, phrases, and terms that seemed alien to him. He felt like a fish out of water, even though he had had a stellar career in the navy. He only found a temporary project or two after looking for nearly a year. Floundering, he seemed unable to secure any permanent position, and was discouraged about how to correct the situation.

Being a commander was his identity and once Michael left the navy, he felt insecure and uncertain about *who* he was. Yet all he needed to do was simply redefine *Brand Michael*. The talents he used daily in the military also had merit in the civilian world. His first step was to clearly identify the specific strengths he had, and then consider jobs where he'd be able to utilize those skills. He focused on a public works director job and a city engineer position. As we closely evaluated his talents and past accomplishments, *Brand Michael* took shape.

STEP 1: Your Brand Equity

Identify your key talents.

His strengths, accomplishments, core competencies, and experience included the following:

- project management with large, complex public works contracts
- well-organized
- analytical
- planner
- good coach, building productive teams
- resourceful problem solver

- excellent budget skills and mind for numbers
- an eye for detailed inspections for quality assurance
- collaborative leadership

STEP 2: Your Brand Advantage

Define your core competency work strengths.

- large scale project management
- planning
- problem solving
- collaborative leadership

List no less than three work accomplishments that you are proud of.

- Directed the regional public works operations for multiple locations with a $200-million annual budget; received Outstanding Job Performance Award.
- Served as project manager on new construction of a $67-million facility, working as owner liaison to construction contractor and overseeing all aspects of the entire project.
- Managed new construction of an $86-million office/medical research facility from conception through design and completion of extensive site preparation involving demolition, environmental remediation, street realignment, utilities relocations, shoring, and dewatering. Delivered on time and on budget.
- Outstanding Job Performance Awards, U.S. Navy Civil Engineer Corps, 1989, 1994, 1998, 2000, 2003

List education, degrees, and special training you have.

Master's of Engineering Degree, Construction Management, University of Florida, Gainesville, 1990
Bachelor of Science Degree, Civil Engineering, University of Virginia, 1982

Master of Arts, National Security and Strategic Studies, United
　　States Naval War College, 1995

STEP 3: Your Brand Passion and Brand Values

Managing projects and building/renovating facilities
Took great pride in his work.

STEP 4: Your Brand Essence

Describe your personality.

- resourceful problem solver
- persuasive
- detail orientated
- friendly, extroverted
- well organized
- analytical
- likeable

STEP 5: Your Brand Image

Define your professional image and outward appearance.

Michael followed my suggestions and, with the help of a
personal shopper, he bought himself a new wardrobe of two suits,
several pairs of dress pants, dress shirts, and ties. The clothing
was conservative yet contemporary. He also maintained some of
his outdoor gear since he might occasionally need to work outside
overseeing construction projects.

STEP 6: Your Brand Reputation

Describe other people's perceptions of you.

It was after reviewing his past performance evaluations and acknowledging his awards that Michael was able to see his value and unique personal brand. A workaholic, he stayed until the job was done right. He was seen as the guy who gets things done, a former supervisor explained.

STEP 7: Your Brand Workplace

Define the workplace environment where you flourish and are most productive.

Governmental organizations or municipalities.

LAST STEP

Write out a brief Brand You *concisely linking all of the steps above, or create a mind map.*

To articulate *Brand Michael,* we created a very strong resumé. This process helped him better understand how his military skills fit in the civilian world. He got an extensive lesson on phrases and buzzwords to use with employers, as well as military jargon to *not* use. Here is the "Summary of Qualifications" section from his resumé, that really captured employers' attention.

CAREER OBJECTIVE: **Public Works Director or City Engineer**

SUMMARY OF QUALIFICATIONS

Award-winning public works administrator and facilities/new construction project manager with twenty years' experience and a proven track record of delivering large-scale projects on time, meeting or coming in under budget, with the highest quality possible. Possesses excellent global overview with keen eye to deciphering problems and implementing workable solutions. Expertise in taking over chaotic and problematic projects and producing goal-meeting results. Recognized for exceptional communication skills, and as superior team builder, working hard to develop individual team members to create highly productive teams.

What Happened to Michael?

With his new insight about his career identity and the ability to more clearly promote his personal brand, Michael's resumé secured him several interviews. We practiced for his interviews and eventually selected one of three job offers, that of city engineer for a large suburban community with a salary of more than $90,000 and a nice bonus option attached. He was very pleased that once he knew how to communicate *Brand Michael*, multiple employers saw his talents, value, and worth.

SHARON—The Reentering Job Seeker

Sharon had worked in a library as a researcher and library aid a dozen years ago. When her son was hurt in a car accident, she became his primary caregiver. After being out of the workplace that long, she finally had to return to work because she needed health and retirement benefits. Sharon wanted to go back into the library world, but she'd been gone a long time and positions were scarce, especially with recent budget cuts. She had no resumé and so we began by discussing her past experiences, old work responsibilities, and volunteer services. We also spent time determining her innate strengths. They included the following:

- excellent researcher
- orderly
- organized
- customer-service oriented
- quiet and polite but friendly
- speed filer
- attention to detail
- good record keeper
- supervising others
- handling statistical data with ease

Despite being out of the professional workforce for twelve years, she had extensive Internet research experience (albeit all unpaid). We created a resumé that substantiated her previous work and volunteer experience. But it was networking that got her in the door at several libraries. She extensively prepared for and practiced interview questions. Her pleasing personality, helpful nature, reliability, and knowledge won her a part-time position with benefits. A new chapter in her life was under way.

MATHEW—The Reinvention of a Been-There-Forever Employee

Repositioning yourself when you've been at the same company for a long time and feel you've reached a plateau is challenging for many. Matt worked as a meter man and a lineman for the power utility company. He had ten years' experience, but no hope of promotion as his current job was a lineman supervising lead. At that level, he had reached the end of the opportunities in his department of the power company. He had been satisfied that this was his job and he did it well, but was at a career dead end. He did some college course work and found he loved all the electronic subjects but not the humanities. Slowly he pursued a degree a few courses a year.

He hadn't completed his college program when he became a client of mine. It was his wife that urged him to consider applying for a trainer position in the technical area for his power company. He asked his boss, a former boss, and the human resources manager, and they all encouraged his application but advised him that the lack of a degree and no past trainer experience were significant obstacles to overcome.

We explored his talents. Matt was a mechanically gifted individual. He had a knack for fixing problems with electrical equipment and meters that stumped others. He also enjoyed teaching the department's new hires about the power company's metering, electrical, and safety issues. Still, he was reluctant to apply for the training position for fear of rejection and almost didn't, but I encouraged him, believing he did stand a decent chance.

Matt had never had a resumé before, so creating *Brand Mathew* was a valuable guide for him. We examined his innate strengths, and writing these down made him realize he did indeed have a lot more to offer. His talents included being:

- mechanically adept
- talented at repairing equipment
- safety oriented
- conscientious
- thorough
- analytical
- methodical
- able to explain circuits and electricity to others

The position paid well, in the mid- to upper seventies, so many internal and external candidates applied. Mathew's cover letter stressed his years of hands-on experience in the field, his lead supervisor experience, and the informal occasions where he'd taught other meter men or linemen who were new to the company. His image was an important part of his brand. It was a balancing act of appealing to the blue collar workers that he'd be teaching and, being a fit for the upper echelon because he'd now be classified as part of the training office, which was management. We decided a suit would not work. He would need to do demonstrations for much of the training, so we selected khaki Dockers pants and a nice-looking polo shirt. It was the ideal choice to fit both worlds.

We spent alot of our consulting time grooming him for the internal interview. After three interviews, Matt got the position, and with it he moved into the management ranks. Many of his peers were astounded that he made such a transition, but his personal brand had all the necessary elements to show he'd be a good fit for the job. He's done well in the position, gotten several raises, and just a few months ago he was promoted to senior technical trainer. Matt demonstrated that you never have to languish at one level at one company. There is always room for growth and greater rewards if you apply yourself and look into new areas.

As we've seen in this chapter, *Brand You* can be successfully applied to many different career situations. Turn to page 141 and begin to reinvent your unique life.

> "*The greatest waste in the world is the difference between what we are and what we could become.*"

BEN HERBSTER,
seventeenth-century British poet

PART 3

CREATING *BRAND YOU*

> *Believe in yourself! Have faith in your abilities!*
> *Without a humble but reasonable confidence*
> *in your own powers you cannot be*
> *successful or happy.*

NORMAN VINCENT PEALE

CHAPTER 8

BRAND IMAGE

irst and foremost, your brand should be about your skillset and inherent talents—qualities that come from the inside. It must be said, however, that the outside does matter, and others notice how you present yourself to the world. People should take a moment and ask themselves: what do I wear to work? This should be a key question these days, when anything goes. Or does it?

"Employees seem to be absolutely clueless when it comes to dressing for work," said Wendy Lovell, an exasperated HR director. "I want to turn some of our employees in to the fashion police. Too many people—young and old alike—have lost touch with what casual dress means. Many employees come to work looking like slobs. Sexy, sluttish, wrinkled, or filthy clothes have no place at work, despite what many people believe. None of those types of attire meet dress code standards, yet we see employees dress that way every day. And while I may not be on the leading edge of fashion, I think wearing the exact same pants and T-shirt *every* workday is gross, yet we've got some guys here that do just that."

It does seem that there are a whole lot of workers out there who just aren't thinking. Spandex. Nose rings. Blue hair. Huge, baggy tops. T-shirts with obscenities on them. Stilettos. Low-rider jeans with belly buttons or butt cracks showing. Slippers. Micro miniskirts. Underwear as outerwear. Body art. Fishnet stockings. Gothic makeup. Braless. Flip-flops. The work taboo list keeps shrinking.

"Expecting the employer to accept you as you are is a terrific attitude if you never want a promotion, or hope that we'll never hire you," said HR director Tracy White. "I often tell our employees, when it comes to work dress, if you look in the mirror and question anything, change your clothes. Likewise, if you return home from a day on the job and you don't have to change clothes to go out, you've dressed too sloppy or too sexy."

Heated discussions go on inside HR departments and senior executives' offices on what is appropriate and what is not. *USA Today* recently wrote a cover page article entitled "How Not to Dress for Work." The experts, executives, and HR directors all seemed in agreement that a reversal trend is now upon us, moving the workplace away from business casual to business formal. Employees had gone way too far. A key worry was insulting or offending others, particularly customers, with inappropriate clothing selection. Ineffectiveness and threats to productivity also worry bosses. And a major concern was how some outfits could, and had, led to sexual harassment suits.

Managers often fumble with their own embarrassment when they need to tell an employee that his or her clothes are too sexy, sloppy, or downright inappropriate for work. In light

Additional image-building tips to help you to be viewed positively in today's workplace include:

- Get a contemporary hairstyle that looks stylish, professional, and appropriate for your age as a working woman and not a college-kid look.
- Dress stylishly—nothing baggy, sexy, sloppy-looking, grungy, or transparent.
- Skirt length should be just above the knee, to the knee, or slightly below, or to ankle if in style.
- Wear classic shoes (not sneakers) and match to your outfits.
- Keep your jewelry simple. Multiple earrings and face- or body-piercing jewelry are not appropriate for work.
- Makeup should be light and enhance your natural beauty.
- Go easy on the fragrance.

Remember, artistic expression can be *creative* without being repulsive or offensive.

If you are a woman in your midcareer, or are at the stage when you want to reinvent yourself, create a look that's uniquely yours, not a duplicate of someone else's. Careless, washed out, frumpy, sloppy, old-fashioned, or shoddy are the looks most employers reported and criticized in this age group. You are more likely to be a manager or professional at this stage, with more responsibility and often more interaction with senior management and customers. You become a role model to subordinates and younger workers, and you need to take great care to present a professional image!

If you are a part of the corporate echelon, be a role model for the organization—always look the part of the successful but approachable executive. A business suit is appropriate for all business situations. I can't stress enough the importance of making sure your clothing fits well. Don't pull some suit out of the closet that is ten years old and two sizes too small for a special business event. To best promote your brand, be sure your power suit is well tailored and in a color in which you look vibrant. Matching pantsuits are also great work clothes and you should have several in your wardrobe.

For most workplaces the everyday look could be a nice jacket or blouse with dress slacks or a skirt.

As we age into our forties and fifties, our bodies change and so does our facial coloring. You must create the image of an energetic woman. A few changes may be in order. Restyling your hair and adding color can make you look more vital, youthful, and professional. Makeup should be soft and natural. If you are over fifty avoid the common short-cropped hairdo older women sometimes select, which can make you look old, harsh, and less flexible or approachable. A contemporary hairstyle that is soft and feminine is the look you should strive to achieve.

A word of caution: many women say they don't care much about their appearance, and once they are past their thirties, many really don't. That is until they lose their job and need to find another or don't get the promotion. Then the reality of all that competition—younger applicants with great track records—is very apparent. Make *Brand You* memorable. If you ever need a job, you want your Brand Image to be an asset, not a liability or obstacle that will hold you back. Portray yourself as progressive, as a contributing, energetic, productive employee. It will ensure lifetime success.

Here are some tips for every women to ensure a professional look in today's workplace:

- Dress fashionably in classic clothes that are age appropriate and fit nicely. Forget anything that is trendy, baggy, frumpy, sloppy, matronly, skin-tight, transparent, or sexy; no jeans or T-shirts.

- You can enhance your looks by coloring your hair. Keep it up and do not allow telltale grow-out lines.
- Long hair can reveal your age. Wear a contemporary, feminine, and sophisticated hairstyle.
- A great-fitting business suit is a closet staple. Select colors that make you look and feel attractive.
- Everyday attire may include: pantsuits, blazer and jacket, or blouse and sweater with dress slacks or a skirt. Skirt length should be just above the knee, to the knee, or slightly below. Blouses and sweaters should not be tight, revealing, or baggy.
- Wear your cutesy clothes (such as the Santa Claus sweater) in your off-work hours.
- Wear nice-looking, well-polished shoes, not scuffed or worn out; no sneakers.
- Match shoes to your suit and dress outfits.
- Clothes should fit comfortably, so it's easy to move around and work, but be tailored for a classic look.
- Keep your jewelry stylish but simple.
- Makeup should be light and enhance your features. Avoid anything that makes you look pasty or with too stark a contrast to your skin, such as deep red lipstick on a pale face.
- Get a manicure (even if you don't polish your nails) for a classy look.

A Tip for Everyone

Smile often—your warm smile always makes you look confident and competent.

Consider a Makeover to Enhance *Brand You.*

Look in the mirror before you leave for your job. If you search your closet and don't find clothes that look good on you, it's time to head out to the mall, or even look online, and invest in a wardrobe that's going to fit *Brand You.* You are striving for a sharp, pulled-together image.

> Note below any changes you want to consider in order to communicate the message you want to project.
>
> Wardrobe
>
>
> Personal appearance
>
>
> If you need to go shopping, what will you look for?

If you are an up-and-coming employee, your image needs to reflect to upper management that you are a capable and business-savvy employee that the company needs on their leadership team. Dress up, not down. This will enhance your personal brand.

SPECIAL ADVICE ON IMAGE PRESENTATION FOR MEN

YOUR IMAGE, CLOTHES, and style are scrutinized and judged by other workers, bosses, colleagues, and potential hiring groups. Dress appropriately for the organization and the promotion that you may want to get someday. *Brand You* suffers if you don't dress for success.

HR managers and senior executives often say that men's definition of casual dress clothes has, unfortunately, degraded into sloppy, wrinkled, baggy, dirty, obscene, ill-fitting, and even ripped clothing as acceptable work attire. If any of these words define what you wear, a makeover is absolutely necessary if you wish to advance your career, and move up or on. Keep this fact in mind: in your working lifetime you'll likely have eleven job changes. Some of these changes are by choice, some result from a layoff or firing. Either way, these changes will force you to compete with the rest of the world for a new position. At those times, your brand image will take on critical importance.

RULE OF THUMB: DRESS *UP* FOR WORK.

FOR MEN IN management here are some important guidelines to observe:

- Own classic suit(s), well tailored with perfect fit—not too snug or too loose. Choose a good quality fabric that looks rich. Blues and grays are the power colors that are most appealing on men, so either is a smart choice. Match socks to the color of your suit and your shoes.
- Wear nice-looking, well-polished, dress shoes, no sneakers.
- Business casual should be dress pants—no jeans! Keep a blazer at work so you can transition from casual to a more polished look for an unexpected event.
- Be impeccably groomed—pay special attention to your hands and nails because other people really do notice.
- Wear fresh, clean, and nicely pressed dress, oxford, or polo shirts—solid or with conservative stripes. Choose flattering colors.
- Wear conservative—not wild—ties with dress shirts to give a more professional, businesslike image.
- Have a contemporary, conservative hairstyle without gels

or the greasy kid stuff. Short, nicely trimmed hair always looks best. No hats or baseball caps on the job even if you are hiding that you have lost, or are losing your hair.

- Be clean shaven, every day. If you elect to wear a beard or mustache, keep it well trimmed; researchers have reported that more than 70% of interviewers and top management do not like heavy facial hair on their employees.
- Wear body jewelry only in your off-hours, not in the workplace

For everyday wear, copy the professional look of your senior managers. You need to look like a person who is going places and be viewed as the promotable type. Nice pants and dress shirts or polo shirts are acceptable, but leave the T-shirts and jeans at home. It is *never* appropriate to wear T-shirts with profanity or suggestive slogans to the workplace.

For your everyday casual but professional look, take the following steps:

- Make sure you are impeccably groomed—pay special attention to your hands and nails because other people really do notice.
- Wear fresh, clean—not wrinkled or baggy—dress or polo shirts. Wear flattering colors.
- Keep a tie at work for a quick, professional upgrade.
- Wear dress pants, Dockers, pressed cords, or linen or wool slacks—not jeans.
- Have a contemporary but conservative hairstyle.
- Be clean shaven every day.
- Smile often—a warm smile always makes you look better.

A word of advice on job interviews: do not dress casually for the promotional or new job interview no matter how casual a prospective company's office environment might seem. It sends the message that you are nonchalant or lackadaisical in all you do. That is *not* the brand image of the successful, talented person who is a vital contributor that you want the employer to remember. Invest in a well-fitted, conservative suit. You'll need it for important work events and job interviews. A navy blue suit is a good choice. For a dress shirt, a pale color sometimes enhances your look, for example, pale blue instead of stark white. Select a conservative tie. Do not wear sneakers; wear dress shoes and socks that match the suit. Skip the earrings. Play close attention to your hygiene—clean hair and nails. Light cologne is best used sparingly.

If you are in your early career or are twentysomething, it's often hard to make that transition from student to professional. Sloppy, wrinkled, or baggy clothes seem to be the biggest fashion crimes for men in this group. And if your focus is to advance your career, you may need to seriously amend your image and wardrobe to better position yourself for promotions and terrific assignments. Look around and find some role models who are company stars. Emulate their professional dress. Employers hate the grunge look. It is widely considered to be a career anchor, not a career asset. A fashionable haircut and appropriate clothing will go a long way toward redefining the professional you.

Most offensive: obscenities on clothing, baggy or soiled clothes, exposed body art and piercings, tattered jeans and ragged sneakers, and the three-day unshaved look.

If you are in your thirties or forties, consider that many men lose their athletic fitness as they age. Bellies grow disproportionately and weight creeps up. Look for clothes that compliment, not accentuate, any weight problem. One client said he had overheard two senior VPs talking about a promotion he desperately wanted. When his name came up he cringed when one VP said, "Forget him, he's a heart attack waiting to happen." Work to create an image of energy and vitality.

Men who've been laid off often find it ego shattering. Several male clients in their forties and fifties have expressed to me how worried they were about not being able to compete and land a new job when going up against younger applicants. Many of these men told me that it was the fear of not getting hired again that had been their motivation for going on a diet and hitting the gym on a daily basis.

ANALYZE YOUR IMAGE TO ENHANCE *BRAND YOU*

LOOK IN THE mirror before you leave for your job. If you search your closet and don't find clothes that look good on you, it's time to head out to the mall or even look online, and invest in a wardrobe that's going to fit *Brand You*. You are striving for a business-savvy, pulled-together look. Ask for help if you're not talented in this area. Many women or store clerks can guide you in the right direction.

> Note below any changes you want to consider in order to communicate the message you want to project.
>
> Wardrobe
>
>
> Personal appearance
>
>
> If you need to go shopping, what will you look for?

Updating or reinventing yourself may be easier than you think. A changed and improved you is always an asset to getting hired or promoted. Presentation and image mistakes can derail your future success. People *notice* how you dress and, sadly, make stereotyped characterizations based on limited knowledge. You can't change the world but you *can* change and polish up your image. Your goal: make your personal grooming and dress look the part of the successful, contemporary, promotable man, so *Brand You* is positively memorable.

FEELING GOOD FROM THE INSIDE OUT

THERE IS A certain healthy radiance that you can spot in a person who makes taking good care of their health a priority. As we age, looking, feeling, and being healthy becomes increasingly important. And, when we don't look or feel healthy, it lowers the value of *Brand You*.

Taking care of your health is easier said than done. The mantra for many workers today is, "I'm so stressed out." While some stress is expected in our jobs, too much stress decreases our productivity and will also jeopardize our health. Being overcommitted is often the culprit behind feeling stressed out. Having too much to do to with too little time to get it done, compounded by outside obligations such as family needs, daycare schedules, lack of sleep, social and personal duties plus your children's activities, can make you hyperventilate with anxiety. It's good to remember that every person has the same twenty-four hours in any one day. There are many time management books and simplify-your-life-approaches that you could read and implement. There are all kinds of miracle cures from $7,000 spa trips to the latest get-fit-quick diet. We can all get overwhelmed, particularly because as we age our personal demands usually grow right along with our work demands. The most common complaint that I hear from clients (and I've said it myself) is, "I have no time to exercise or even to eat well." The short-term result is that we skate by, but in the long term we may pay a much higher price such as a serious illness or a dying career.

Reserving some personal time and energy each day is key

to maintaining your health and enhancing your inner radiance. Here are the best ways to watch the stress and achieve this well-being:

- exercise
- maintain a healthy diet
- get rest and relaxation
- find some ME time

Relaxation, seven to eight hours of sleep per night, and enjoying personal time, whether it is reading, listening to music, or communing with nature, all add to your health and well-being. Be sure that wellness is high on your *Brand You* list.

In summary, your personal presentation—appearance, clothes, and mannerisms—has a very profound effect on others. *Brand You* and your Brand Image must be congruent to present the best you possible when you head off to work.

> *To accomplish great things, we must not only act, but also dream; not only plan, but also believe.*
>
> **—ANATOLE FRANCE,**
> novelist

CHAPTER 9

CREATE *BRAND YOU* FOR *YOU*

ow it's time to finally create *Brand You* for *you*! You've already read about how others have taken a good look at themselves, realized who they are and what they have to offer, and created an external tool that helped them express their value to others. And once they did this, they changed their lives for the better. As we've seen, the process is broken down into several easy steps, so let's get started and create *Brand You*!

STEP 1: Your *Brand Equity*

Identify your key talents and unique strengths. (These were noted in chapter two.)

-
-
-
-
-
-
-

STEP 2: Your *Brand Advantage*

Define your core competency work strengths.

Narrow your focus and select a couple areas you have mastered into core competencies. Do not try to be all things to all people. No one believes you if you say that you are. Just as one leader may excel in strategic planning as a core competency another excels in leading and motivating employees resulting in increased productivity. The more concentrated, the more specialized, the easier *Brand You* is recognized by others.

My key core competencies are:

Core competencies must yield results. Employers focus on what you get—or don't get—accomplished, so be very specific in your noted accomplishments.

List no less than five work accomplishments that you are proud of.

1.
2.
3.
4.
5.

List education, degrees, and special training or honors you have.

STEP 3: Your Brand Passion and Brand Values

Define your passions, driving interests, and important values.

STEP 4: Your Brand Essence

List no less than five (up to ten) personality traits.

1.	6.
2.	7.
3.	8.
4.	9.
5.	10.

STEP 5: Your Brand Image

Define your professional image and outward appearance. Note assets and any improvements that need to be made.

STEP 6: Your Brand Reputation

Write down other people's perceptions of you. If you aren't sure, ask!

Note: Who are your top work references?

STEP 7: Your Brand Workplace

Define the workplace environment where you flourish and are most productive.

LAST STEP

Choose one, two, or do all three of the following.

1. Write out *Brand You* in one concise paragraph that includes your strengths, personality traits, core competencies, image, and others' perceptions of you and your work. You should also try to incorporate the environment or culture in which you seem to flourish.

2. Create a *Brand You* resumé.
3. Make a *Brand You* mind map.

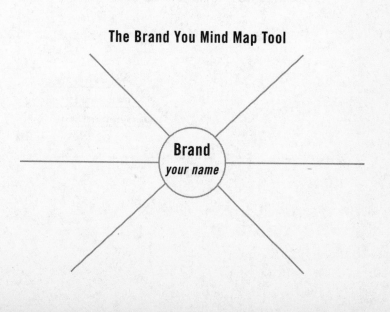

The Brand You Mind Map Tool

Brand
your name

Here are some tips on creating your mind map.

This visual tool is used primarily to lay out your strengths, to make them easy to recall and discuss. When you begin your map you may find hand drawing more appealing than this solid-line, computer-made map. Creative types enjoy using colored markers to make curvy lines that look like tree branches. (Additional examples of mind maps can be viewed on www.BrandYouKit. com.) For the purposes of our examples in this book we're going to use black lines and words, but use whatever style works for you. Keep in mind that your objective is to clearly and concisely define the authentic you. Using the spokes on the map, write down key words to describe *Brand You* for each of the areas below:

- In the center of the mind map write your first name and put a circle around it.
- Define one of your strengths, talents, or areas of unique knowledge using a couple of keywords on one of the spoke lines in the mind map. For example, list how many years of experience you have in a particular field.

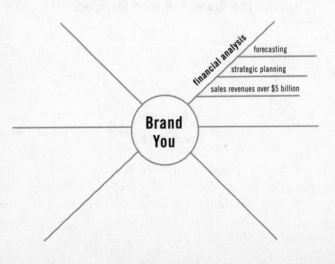

- Write another strength on the next spoke. Examples include: project manager, writer, financial team leader, strategic planner, and so on.
- Now identify three or four more key talents for a grand total of five or six on your mind map. Be sure that these are core competencies.
- Now examine your headings. You may want to add some keywords as offshoots.

BETA TEST *BRAND YOU*

YOU NEED TO determine if others see you as you see yourself. You should ask your boss or chairman, a colleague or two, an HR director, or a staff person how they see you. Take the completed mind map of your personal brand to several people and ask them if it is accurate or if you've missed anything important. This prevents a devaluation of your skills, a sin many people are guilty of. Too many times people fail to acknowledge their key gifts. They ignore or devalue their talents. Often others can more easily see and recognize your strengths. This step is important to get a true handle on all the areas in which you excel.

Don Essig, who wrote *Personal Excellence for Key People,* often speaks about discovering your strengths. He insists we all need "data feedback." This is a system in which we collect information, verify whether or not it is true, do something with the information, and evaluate our actions. Most important, it involves the old cliché, In case of doubt, check it out!

Indeed, this exercise can be eye-opening. Although you can't guarantee complete frankness, if you ask people to be forthright and not protective of your feelings, you'll get the information you need. Many times our perceptions of how we think people view us is quite different from the way they actually see us. Knowing the reality of how others see us is a very important part of clarifying *Brand You.* Don't skip this crucial step.

Once completed, you have a road map for creating *Brand You.* There is no right or wrong way to define yourself. You will add to or change the map over time. But with this visual tool it is much easier for you to recognize yourself as the special, unique individual that is the essence of you.

In summary, you have now created your own distinctive, one-of-a-kind career identity and personal brand. Accomplishments, core competencies, and strengths have been clearly defined. Now it's time to learn how to make it work for you so you can improve your future.

PART 4

IMPLEMENTING *BRAND YOU*

> *" The average person puts only 25 percent of his energy and ability into his work. The world takes off its hat to those who put in more than 50 percent of their capacity, and stands on its head for those few and far between souls who devote 100 percent. "*

ANDREW CARNEGIE,
industrialist and one of
the wealthiest men of his time

CHAPTER 10

BRAND YOU AND PROMOTIONS

rand You can create an opportunity for you to excel in a job you love, by linking your enthusiasm, interests, and expertise with your potential. It's not only a method to define and realize your goals but also a way to ensure you will be highly valued, retained, and promoted. You want a position you're passionate about and your boss and company want a star employee who is great at the job. In a Pollyanna world, that would be the perfect win-win equation. But you live in the real world, which has dysfunctional employers, irrational bosses, and good fits and poor ones. Sometimes these challenges make you feel as though the only way you will be happy is to move on. But many leave too quickly, believing that the grass will be greener elsewhere. The fact is you may be sitting on a goldmine right in your current workplace.

Russell Conwell (1843–1925) was a gentleman who traveled around the United States preaching to people about the importance of nurturing opportunities right in front of them. Dr. Conwell wanted to build a college to educate smart, ambitious men who had no means to pay for their education. It was his life's passion. Needing millions of dollars for his cause, Dr. Conwell traveled around the country telling the Acres of Diamonds tale, a true story with an ageless moral, in order to raise funds.

The story began in Africa, with a man named Ali, who had been blessed with a large farm but still wished for greater wealth. As a result, he spoke to the village priest for guidance and the sage advised him to look for a river with white sands. It was there that Ali would find many valuable diamonds. So this farmer, dreaming of a fortune in precious gems, sold his farm to wander the continent in search of treasures. Years slipped by as Ali went from river to river, but he found no diamonds. Eventually, completely broke, he drowned himself.

Meanwhile, one day the new owner of Ali's farm noticed an unusual looking rock about the size of a large egg down by the edge of the river on his land. He took it home and put it on his mantle as a curiosity piece. A visitor stopped by and upon seeing the rock on the mantle, exclaimed, "This is a diamond. I think it may be the biggest diamond that has ever been found." The new owner of the farm said, "Heck, the whole farm is covered with them." And sure enough, it was. The farm became the Kimberly Diamond Mine—the richest the world has ever known. Ali had been literally standing on "Acres of Diamonds" until he sold his farm.

Dr. Conwell's Acres of Diamonds story both moved and inspired people, so he included it in more than six thousand lectures. He had kept his own dream and purpose in mind, that of wanting to provide a place where the poor could get a quality education. He eventually raised millions of dollars and founded Temple University, serving as its first president for thirty-eight years.

Too many people are searching for greener pastures. And too often people quit just before they could have made it big. That's a common career mistake that you should try to avoid. Some folks trade jobs every few years looking for career nirvana, but never stick around long enough to achieve it where they are.

The metaphors in the farmer's story are powerful and thought-provoking. Instead of envying what you don't have, concentrate on developing what you do have. The universe does not make mistakes. Don't abandon your strengths and undeveloped talents by taking a road that is not your true path or destiny. Those who build on their strengths are usually life's most successful people. Those who ignore their talents are frequently dissatisfied. Look at all the opportunities around you to improve the job you now have or to move within your organization. *Brand You* can help you realize that you may be sitting on your own acre of diamonds.

In our modern-day world, here is how a client dug for treasure in her own backyard. Lauren started her career as a secretary for a nonprofit organization. She learned a great deal from her boss, and made some important contributions. She was promoted to program coordinator, a new job the company created just for her. Lauren did not have a degree, but was very active in professional associations and she attended numerous seminars on program management, membership development, event planning, and marketing. So although she had not previously performed some of the tasks in her new job, her quest to learn and better herself allowed her to excel. She developed her career by establishing her brand as a person who excelled at strategic planning, who could effectively grow programs and be relied upon to get things done efficiently and correctly the first time. She produced results and her organization grew because of her efforts. Then Lauren reached a point where she felt her current career had plateaued. She didn't see any more moves up in her small organization. She got bored with her work and eventually decided to look elsewhere for something more challenging. We met after she had applied for a couple of jobs with no results.

Listening to her discuss, with such pride, the organization she'd help build, I advised her that reinventing her career where she was might be a better option than leaving the company. We reviewed her strengths and I suggested she talk to her boss about how she might better apply them within her current organization. She did her homework and had solid suggestions for her boss. She successfully showed him how her strengths could better benefit them, and the executive director created a new, higher level position just for her. She continues to thrive, enjoying the promotion and the nice raise it brought.

WHAT DOES YOUR IDEAL JOB LOOK LIKE?

IN ORDER TO create *your* dream job, some job assessment is in order. You need to consider these key questions:

- Are you using your best talents at your current job?
- If no, why not?
- What do you like and enjoy at your job?
- What do you dislike?
- What would you like the opportunity to do more of?

- Can you brainstorm about ways to ask for more work you enjoy and at which you excel, and find ways to trade out tasks you are bored by or you don't like doing?

List the tasks and activities that you would like to undertake more often.

Define clearly your ideal dream job including duties, boss, perks, and company environment.

To create the dream position where you are, note the people who can help you; the action needed to achieve it; your timeline to reach those goals. My plan is:

As you plan your future, remember Lauren's promotion came from her ability to rethink her job and focus on utilizing her strengths for the benefit of her company. She also developed a good working relationship with her boss and her boss's boss. The strengths of Lauren's brand derived from her association work, her networking efforts, and her continuous improvement and use of all her talents. Note what improvements you can initiate to help your organization save time, increase revenues, or improve efficiency or the bottomline.

REDESIGNING YOUR JOB

SOMETIMES IT'S BEST to admit that you are not good at a certain task and you should examine options within your organization to better align your strengths and your work assignments. This is a self-assessment task that you begin on your own but then take to your boss or another company manager if you would be moving under another's supervision. Create a list in which you outline strengths and related tasks. Your goal is to undertake more of the activities that match your strengths and either eliminate or reassign the tasks at which you are weak or that you find hard. Your boss is a vital player if this is to happen. Before you make requests, document in writing the changes you suggest that will allow you to use more of your strengths and state *how* they will result in improvements that will benefit the company.

For example: Mark was a methodical person and excelled at researching data and compiling it in a useful manner. This was not a task required in his job, but one he liked and did whenever needed. We met when he was thinking of leaving.

Instead, we evaluated his job and developed a chart showing the tasks, such as marketing research, and the results he could achieve: appropriate lists and prospecting niches for the sales team. Although, his strengths were in research, he had been assigned various writing and client contact tasks in which he was not proficient. He brought the idea to his boss, pointing out the weaker areas that a coworker could do better. His boss admitted that Mark's weaker communication skills were preventing him from greater success. His boss agreed to a two-month trial period. Several department heads were impressed with Mark's research results. He got a promotion as a result of this permanent change, with a new title and a raise.

Mark's initiative and effort paid off. He brought his idea to several marketing and sales directors inside the company to build consensus. This all came from *his efforts*. His promotion was a direct result of defining *Brand Mark*, delivering excellent results, and being memorable to the powers above. Many times a redesigned job becomes your promotion, one where you initiate the whole process, instead of waiting or hoping someone above you will come up with an idea.

To float an idea, create a thorough, one page, executive summary to review with your boss, or even HR, as an outline for the conversation.

Contrary to what you may think, most managers want their employees to succeed because having successful employees reflects well on them. If you show management how the company would benefit from your improved performance by taking on a new duty or two (and/or letting go of those that don't utilize your talents), it will most likely be well received and the suggested changes will be implemented.

CEO Melinda Howard, author of the book *Work Smart*, offers this sage advice: "Be open with your boss and communicate your goals. Be sure you understand what the boss sees as the priorities and what his goals are. You both need to be on the same page! To change things, simply ask for what you want. Take the initiative. Make suggestions about the tasks you'll undertake or the improvements you think you can make. It is taking the initiative that is often the key to obtaining a job that you're going to enjoy every single day."

Managers love employees who seek out new training, so try to become a lifelong learner. Continually improve yourself and strive to master and excel in your talents. The world is constantly changing so you may have to adjust your skills and learn new ones that complement your strengths. Experiment and try different things. It's not wise or practical, though, to deviate into areas you feel you can't master. Focus on personal self-development in areas where you can excel and become a true expert.

Those who take initiative and volunteer to take on more tasks and play to their strengths are the ones who solidify *Brand You* in the minds of others.

Define five tasks to undertake that will improve your job with your current employer.

Designate three things to personally work on to improve yourself or learn in the next year. Note the details of how you will accomplish this.

Samantha, who was a vice president at a large company, discussed the problem of career success and attrition. Her company had experienced the loss of a lot of employees who were convinced that faster promotions and raises were to be found elsewhere. She noted that in many fields, it was the nature of the industry for people to move around a lot. "Many employees don't realize that they have created a reputation for being a job hopper, which really hurts their long-term careers. We, just like many other employers, are looking for individuals who want to make contributions and will stay long enough to do just that. I can't tell you how many executives have said many a worker just doesn't understand that. When we first hire someone we know that the learning curve might be long. We are making a significant investment by paying their salary while that person is actually learning about our company and the job they are supposed to do. For middle management and higher level personnel, that can mean six months to a year before they really have a handle on the position and have really learned the job. We know true accomplishments often come from longevity. That's why it's important to hire people with a strong track record of staying on the job for more than a year or two," this VP advised.

Step back for a minute and consider where you are in your current position and place of employment. I recommend that you take the time to work with your boss, your boss's boss, or the HR department to try to determine the place in your company that is a good fit for you.

The following guidelines will be useful at any point as you navigate your career and develop the dream job within your company.

- Develop a skillset—skills, talents, and experiences.
- Adopt a can-do, *enthusiastic*, attitude that focuses on personal excellence and quality.

- Be results orientated—highly productive, organized, and efficient.
- Continuously acquire new skills.
- Focus your time and energy on success and successful pursuits.
- Develop a reputation for integrity, fairness, and honesty.
- Continuously develop your professional network.
- Be involved in professional organizations and associations in your field.
- Review your career every year and map out an annual plan.
- Perfect your communication skills.
- Believe in yourself, your goals, and the importance of your work.
- Celebrate your victories, big and small.

BETTER OPPORTUNITIES OFTEN COME WITH SMALL EMPLOYERS

SMALL COMPANIES ARE the lifeblood of the workplace. They hire nearly 90% of all workers and it's within their organizations that 75% of all new jobs are created. The small company (five hundred employees or less) offers some terrific opportunities to advance, take on more responsibilities, and get a great deal of broader experience. Oftentimes, if you want to go in a new direction, the best options may be waiting for you there in those smaller organizations. Depending on where you are in your career, you could grow and prosper along with them.

If you are still in the beginning stages of your career, you will advance your skillset much faster by electing to work for a small employer. You'll get broader experience, more guidance, and greater responsibility since the organization's size means everyone has a broader scope of job duties. A small employer can help you fast-track into greater job responsibilities with a larger employer, since your strengths and skills will develop faster. You accomplish more in a shorter time frame than someone at a large *Fortune* 500 company.

Of course, you could ultimately hit the glass ceiling and find that there is no more room to move up. But look closely before you leap to another company and make sure that you have gotten all you can out of your current employment situation.

MISCONCEPTIONS ABOUT PROMOTIONS

MANY EMPLOYEES BELIEVE that they can get a promotion simply because they have been at a company a long while and thus deserve it. Many employees suffer from a sense of entitlement. Yet mangers say, "*Merit* is the yardstick for raises these days. We need to see more results or new skills." Nobody gets to the top without hard work. If you lack the passion or that inner desire to become very competent and known at something, you won't have the Brand Reputation necessary to secure raises or promotions. You can hold any job if your goal is to be the best there is. You need to say, "I'm going to have a strategy for my career. I'm going to foster my career identity. I'm going to plot where I'm going. I'm also going to be open to opportunities because sometimes an opportunity comes along and the career takes another path." Developing a favorable Brand Reputation through a proven track record is essential for obtaining promotions.

Still, many people may be vying for promotions and not everyone can get them. The people that get ahead are not the ones that are *waiting* for the promotion. It just doesn't happen that way. First you've got to be proactive about cultivating your future. Second you have to have an admirable Brand Reputation that showcases your Brand Advantages and proves your worth. When both of these areas work in concert, you have the makings of a highly sought after personal brand that will cata-pult you to the top of any mountain you care to climb!

Still, there are many who believe that if they do a good job, they'll automatically be promoted. Amy was a good cus-tomer service rep working in the call center for a mortgage banker. She called me in tears because she was bypassed and somebody else got promoted to the supervisor level. When asked, "Have you made it clear to your boss how good you are?" she replied with a simple, "He knows." That's what she be-lieved, yet she lacked *facts* on exactly *how* or *what* the boss *did* know. That false assumption cost her the advancement.

Out of college two years, she was a quiet worker bee, a hard worker, but an introverted person. Amy believed that by just doing a good job she'd be noticed and selected for a man-agement promotion. She missed a critical point in career man-agement, and that is the self-promotion of *Brand You*. At this point she had two choices. Promote *Brand You* inside her orga-nization or look for a new job. Either way, she needed to iden-tify her strengths, discuss her professional goals with her boss, and network inside her company. She collaborated with her boss. When a new supervisory position opened, her new re-sumé and cover letter advertised her personal brand, and she practiced to make sure her brand was clearly communicated in the interview. Amy landed the promotion and has been pro-moted twice since then.

John worked in the technical research and development area for Microsoft. After two promotions he was lead tech, re-ceiving continuous praise from his boss for his good work. John had built a great relationship with his supervisor over the five years he'd worked for her. She recognized and acknowledged *Brand John* as having strengths not only on the technology side, which was essential for his job, but in management as well.

John shared his newest goal a few months after his last promotion. He wanted to be a project manager in the Research and Development Division. His boss and an HR manager both confirmed John had gone as far as he could go until he completed some programming courses. They told him that programming knowledge was the essential background he would need to move up into project management. He did not ever need to be a programmer. He only needed the knowledge to be better able to lead the technological team.

John admitted that programming was not his strength. He'd taken an introduction to programming class in college, finding it difficult. He resisted returning to school, but eventually took all the recommended programming courses. His boss noticed; when a new project manager position eventually opened up, she helped John by introducing him to the hiring manager (the job was with another supervisor), coached him on his interview, and was genuinely pleased when he landed the promotion with an extraordinary raise. His boss had recognized *Brand John* noting that his technical understanding with the excellent ability to manage others, coordinate workflow, plan timelines, and schedule work was a key strength that made his career identity stand out. The pièce de résistance, though, was that he proved he was adaptable, a lifelong learner, and willing to take on challenges to stay ahead of the curve. He's excelled in this new position. He's passionate about the job, and he uses his key strengths every day.

HIGH FLYERS GET THE PROMOTIONS

SMART COMPANIES GO out of their way to look for internal employees who will enhance the organization. They label some as stars or high flyers, noting, "We're grooming her for that higher-level position." Needless to say your internal promotion is very dependent on how *Brand You* is viewed by others.

Amazon.com global director of human resources, Wendy McIntosh, has observed the career advances of many people.

She declares that it is the employee who is memorable not only for his strengths and skills, but who also has a discernable passion, who will either get to, or is already at, the top of his profession.

"High flyers produce!" says McIntosh. "Their results scream achievement, instead of just words or rhetoric trying to attest to how good they are. It's other people's perception of your core competencies that influences their opinion of you."

This HR executive offered an example of a woman who personified this concept. Mary was a corporate lawyer at a *Fortune* 100 company. Her key job responsibility at the time was closing big deals for the company as its senior legal negotiator. Mary's top talents were well known throughout the company, and she had established a brand for being the best negotiator and deal maker. She would often quote something her mother had said: "Mary, you were making deals when you were just five years old. I would tell you that you had to drink milk and you'd spend twenty minutes trying to convince me that you should be able to drink a Pepsi instead." *Brand Mary* was well established as someone who was very good at getting whatever she wanted.

Mary had developed her talents as a negotiator long after she had left law school. She was working on contracts, reviewing lengthy documents for compliance or final signing for her company. Often she would find mistakes and contact the other lawyers or executives to clarify and finalize specific points. Her natural strength as a negotiator emerged and the general counsel for the company took notice. She was promoted and then moved up again to the number two position on the negotiating team. Eventually, after several years, she was promoted to the top negotiating job. Mary excelled, and her brand became better known to those inside and outside the company.

When a VP of strategic planning position became available, Mary's CEO hadn't considered her for the job until a vendor whose contracts she frequently worked on recommended her, noting, "She's the person for that job!"

He sure had noticed her talents. Mary's personal brand is transparent to anyone who meets her—strong, direct, a real no-nonsense woman, never missing a detail. She is pure business, not emotional at all, two steps ahead of everyone. She is tough as nails.

The ability to mask your thoughts is often a needed strength in the negotiating and deal-making process, which is why this CEO said he promoted her. He concluded, "I knew we needed Mary. Our partnering deals are challenging—very challenging—but I had no doubt that Mary must be one heck of a poker player and that she would deliver the necessary results. And, indeed, she has." He and the internal team recognized that her skills were perfect for that VP role.

Sooner or later someone is going to rate you, most likely when it comes time to decide on a promotion or raise. They will promote your brand to the powers above. Their comments can influence whether you advance or not. In Mary's case, it was a vendor. Your referral agent could be an executive, an assistant, a former employer, a human resources manager, or a client, or someone who worked underneath you.

Tracy White, human resources director at a large accounting firm, noted that it primarily sees two types of workers. "One employee sees only the narrow scope of their particular job and no opportunities; the other sees a global company picture where opportunity is everywhere. The latter is company focused as opposed to the former who is *me* focused. Small thinkers don't contribute enough to the overall company goal to be highly valued. They are typically the first to go, since they are seen as stable, but not promotable. Instead, it is the global workers who will land the promotions, big titles, and leadership roles, securing a stable future," explained this HR director.

There is a new human resources philosophy called top grading that some companies are adopting. Designed for ranking employees it has managers divide workers into A players, B players, and C players. Amazon.com's Wendy McIntosh explained, "The problem with this top grading system is that you have to look hard at *who* the decision maker is, because grading other people is *very subjective*. Sometimes you can be very talented, but if you are in the unfortunate circumstance that your boss happens to be a C player, oftentimes that label can define you, too." Sadly, you can be very good but still rank as a C player against other team members in this forced ranking model.

So what can you do about it? Understand the politics at play. You may need to establish yourself by networking with other managers and even trying to reach upper management, particularly your boss's boss, to make them aware of your contributions. Offer concrete ideas on improvements. You'll stand a better chance of being promoted, no matter what your boss's performance ranking might be.

David D'Alessandro, former CEO of John Hancock and author of *Career Warfare,* states in his book, "Promotions are usually doled out based on someone's instant assessment of you, à la your personal brand. This means that the single most important thing you can do for your career is to lay the groundwork for an attractive personal brand so that the next time someone powerful does think of your name, that person thinks well of you."

One misstep many people make on the way up is known as burning bridges. Victor Boschini, president of Illinois State University, warns, "Each profession may seem big—but I believe that as you move up in your career you realize how small each really is. It makes no sense to right every wrong you felt in a certain organization on your way out. This almost always comes back to haunt you."

High flyers also need to look at their skillset in terms of their long-term goals. If you want to rise to the top, you'll need to always micromanage your career. Tom McMahon, a former marine, is a tall, athletic, very successful VP of retail operations for Starbucks who has followed this advice. Many have wondered how this military man rose so fast in the corporate world, but when you talk to Tom you quickly realize he looks at his position as a boss to service his workers (not *manage, service*), so they can better serve their customers. We discussed how some people fast-track in a large, growing company (one hundred thousand employees) like Starbucks. McMahon revealed, "With such a high emphasis on productivity these days, generalists are passé. To succeed, a person must develop two or three core competencies (defined as strengths you've excelled in and demonstrated good results). Since you'll likely be on a team, it's the specialty you bring to the team that's important."

McMahon rose at PepsiCo and then went to Starbucks. Having a strong background in organizational development and marketing, he excelled in enhancing his team's performance and continued to deliver impressive team results. He stated that high flyers who race up the success ladder all displayed the following behaviors:

- They are very articulate and easily understood. These people can translate thoughts and ideas. They are able to dumb things down without being condescending, so everyone, companywide, can get it.
- They are specialized in a big way. They are an inch wide but a mile deep. They pick just a few top strengths and do them *very well*.
- They are great problem solvers. They are creative and resourceful at finding workable solutions.
- They are masters of inclusion and connectivity with others. They give each person a sense of belonging as well as making them feel important and necessary to the team. They are experts at working with and through others.
- All are geniuses at collaborating to get things done. They work well across divisions and crossfunctionally. They can get all the players organized and deliver desired results. High flyers must be good at delivering results

through others. It is their ability to influence, organize, and motivate that becomes most critical the higher they rise. After a while, you do all the work through others, and none of it hands-on yourself.

- They are typically generous with credit where credit is due. They demand accountability but ensure that the team has the needed resources to accomplish the goals.

The key for high flyers is to be clear on the goal—the top job—and micromanage your career to ensure that you get there.

In summary, internal promotions come about in one of three ways:

- Your current boss recommends you for a promotion within your department, based on good performance.
- An internal opening with the company offers you an opportunity to transfer into a new department.
- You network with other managers inside your company and initiate your own promotability into a created position.

By establishing a strong career identity—*Brand You*—and networking with your boss and other managers inside the company and demonstrating how your strengths and the results you can achieve will benefit the organization, you will be positioned for recruitment and advancement into a higher-level position.

" Only I can change my life
No one can do it for me. "

CAROL BURNETT,
comedian and actress

CHAPTER 11

THE BOSS AND YOU

our career identity will be greatly influenced by your boss. I hope you are fortunate enough to have a supervisor who fosters her team's professional development. If you establish good communication and a solid work relationship between yourself and your supervisor, it often leads to coaching, mentoring, and strategic information, which in turn leads to promotions and reaching a higher level. Your boss can help or sit back and not care, or even hurt your chances if she doesn't want you to leave the job. Some managers, unfortunately, focus only on their own situation and want to keep a good employee in their current job since they do not want to spend the time or effort to replace them and train someone new.

In general, though, the bottom line is you've got to convey to your boss, future manager, or employer that you've solved problems and produced positive results. If not, when it's time for a promotion, you won't be selected. Work in tandem with your boss to offer ideas, take initiative, and ask for more opportunities to use your strengths. The very first and most important person in your work life who needs to clearly recognize *Brand You* is your boss. Therefore, a clearly defined *Brand You* makes distinguishing yourself from your peers essential.

Step one in your professional advancement is to determine your current boss's agenda.

David D'Alessandro, *Fortune* 500 CEO and author of *Career Warfare* offers this advice. "Like it or not, your boss decides how your accomplishments will be viewed by higher-ups. Even if he or she is an idiot, the power is real so handle him or her carefully. I can tell you that it's smart for you to try to think of yourself as a product—a very expensive one—because at the end of the day, that's exactly what you are to your organization, to your boss, and to your customers. You probably cost the company as much every year as a top-of-the-line Mercedes, and that's how they think of you too. So you'd better deliver the performance expected from a luxury brand because no one wants to own an unreliable Mercedes." Therefore, you must be in sync with what the boss expects from you and what *the boss sees* as the priorities. You will not be evaluated on intentions, desires, or dreams, but rather on your actions and the results you do or do not achieve. It's important you understand and have this self-awareness. It is the key to being able to develop a good relationship with your boss and the people above him or her.

"A big part of your job is to make your boss look good," says Tom McMahon, one of Starbucks' VPs. "That is something you must learn to do if you want to rise in any organization. In turn, he will make sure you benefit, too. That's how the game works in the big leagues." Some call it paying your dues;

some recognize it as a fact of business life. But it is essential you understand and operate this way. Even if you depart from your organization, your boss is a key reference that can help or hinder your obtaining a new position somewhere else.

There are office politics in any workplace situation. A fatal mistake some people make in their organization is failing to understand that the boss oftentimes holds the key to the future. Many employees have committed professional suicide by going around their boss. They easily hop up the chain of command, complaining about their supervisor to the boss's manager. They may win a tiny battle, but they usually lose the war. Typically this maneuver of going over your boss's head causes you to develop a career identity and reputation as being disloyal and untrustworthy. And not only will your boss resent you, upper managers will hold that trait against you. After all, if you bad-mouth one boss, other managers secretly worry that that's exactly what you will do to them if you move up the ladder.

KEY ADVICE FROM CEOS

A NATIONAL SURVEY I conducted of CEOs and top executives asked the question, "How do people advance and move up in their career?" Their responses offered a rare glimpse on how you can rise up in any industry. Many of those surveyed reported that they:

- respect good problem solvers
- want employees who show initiative to get ahead
- expect workers who are proactive and ask for what they need
- need their employees to demonstrate a desire to excel on the job
- want their people to develop good communications with

their current boss and be absolutely clear on the boss's priorities, expectations, and goals for them, the department, and the company

These top execs liked action plans. A key piece of advice was to have a vision for now, next year, and five years out. Also, the ability to not only accomplish your goals, but to set new and even bigger ones was highly regarded. Having a written action plan for how you're going to achieve any goal was rated as important, as was the ability to be clear on the specifics, establish timelines, and identify people you could use as resources to help achieve your goals.

Other points that surfaced from the survey were the ability to make things happen by taking initiative and getting training. Computer and communication skills were rated as being essential in today's workplace. Every one of the leaders surveyed said the best thing to do for self-improvement is to constantly be learning and taking advantage of training opportunities to master the skills necessary for doing the job.

Most important, they noted, you'll be judged, by the results you achieve. In regard to this final point, it is important that you use your strengths to excel in your natural areas of ability. By doing so, it'll be easier to achieve terrific results in whatever you do.

A STRATEGIC PLAN FOR YOUR CAREER

THE BEST WAY to please your boss and be noticed by upper management is to enact whatever actions will produce what most bosses want. These include:

1. Good results. This is critical to be in the position to move ahead.
2. Getting the work tasks done on time. Many managers

don't care about when you do the work, but missing deadlines and being unreliable is a sure career killer.

3. Showing initiative. Taking on new tasks, offering good ideas, especially on problem solving or improving procedures, systems, or processes.

4. Loyalty along with honesty and integrity.

5. Making the boss look good

If you seek to move into upper and senior management you should be able to do the following.

1. Deliver results through others.

2. Recognize that earning money for the organization (or saving the company money) is valued.

3. Be a *resourceful* problem solver.

4. Have integrity in what you say, what you do, and what you promise.

5. Make people want to work for you. You must develop this reputation for leadership if you seek to move up in any organization, because at some point, your ability to do things by yourself becomes meaningless. What counts is whether you can get other people to do the needed work.

These are the work practices that you need to employ everyday on the job. Communicate your goals and accomplishments to your boss. Look for opportunities to lead and suggest implementing something new. When you excel, *Brand You* shines and your achievements reflect positively on your boss, which will improve your relationship.

> What changes do you need to make to be more congruent with this recommendation?

There are many good reasons for maintaining a good relationship with your boss, but this client's story shows you just how important that relationship can be.

Liz had pursued a PhD in health psychology and exercise and sports science with the goal of becoming a college professor. "I was always the black sheep in grad school," she stated. "I seemed to have strengths that were frowned upon and certainly not valued at the university level where the emphasis was on publishing research."

To support herself through her graduate program, Liz worked at a medical clinic and did health assessments to earn some money to cover her bills. As Liz came close to finishing her PhD, she worked with a patient named Peggy, and they chatted about Peggy's company, a managed-care healthcare organization. To Liz's surprise, Peggy called a week later and wanted to interview her for a position developing wellness programs.

Liz noted that her future changed in a major way. "I had planned to be a college professor—that is why I undertook a five-year doctoral program. But I guess I was branding myself before I realized such a thing as personal branding existed. Working at the clinic, I would educate patients and discuss wellness and self-care activities. I was smitten when Peggy offered me a position at a starting salary of $58,000. That was ten thousand more than I'd hoped to make as a beginning professor. I *absolutely flourished* in the corporate world. The academic world that I came from did not value my strengths in creativity, practical applications of science, integration of complex data into easily understood information, developing programs, or research and understanding of marketing and health trends. By honing these gifts I was able to rise quickly in the corporate world," she stated. Now, ten years into her career, Liz has moved on to new companies, and has been repeatedly promoted. Recently, she decided to look for a new job in another city. She called all her old bosses just to see if they knew of any jobs. Peggy was excited to hear Liz was available. Peggy immediately recruited Liz to take on an exciting new position as director of health education for Peggy's company, a major international organization. The position paid well over six figures. Liz owes a great deal of her career success to Peggy and has told her so. But her boss says, "I'm the lucky one, Liz. You are a very talented woman and you put everything you have into building terrific new programs. You'll be a true asset here."

A boss can remain a potential career booster your whole life. Liz hadn't worked for Peggy for eight years but the boss remembered *Brand Liz*.

Below are some guidelines and strategies to create a win-win relationship with your manager.

- **Establish a good working relationship.** Your life at work will be easier if you learn about your boss's personality, work style, family background, and recognize traits and telltale signals so you understand his moods. This insight should then shape your actions, such as knowing when to ask for something and when not to.
- **Seek out a mentor.** Carefully consider the manager you'll answer to before you accept any job offer or promotion. If you already have a boss who isn't a mentor look around the organization for someone who will be. If no one seems appropriate, you may need to cultivate a professional relationship with someone outside the organization who can offer some key advice and guidance. In the early stages of your career, it is especially important to seek out a supportive manager. Working under a good boss, you can learn a great deal that is invaluable. It may be better to take a position with a lower salary if it will give you an opportunity to learn, take on new challenges, or perfect your skills. It may be far more useful to your career than a well-paid position with a lousy boss who simply wants to keep you in your place and has no interest in helping you move ahead.

- **Adjust your communications style to match your boss's.** Some managers like detailed weekly or even daily reports. Some are happier with just an occasional email, others prefer in-person chats. Ask exactly how your boss wants to be kept informed of your progress, and how he expects you to approach solving problems that come up.
- **Both you and your boss must be very clear about your goals and the boss's priorities.** You need to work on having good communication with your boss. Sit down and talk about goals and write out your boss's priorities. Make sure that you're both operating under the same assumptions of what is important. It is better to ask questions so that you get the work done to your boss's liking. You want to do it on time and in the expected sequence. Not doing so will surely result in problems. If you've been given several tasks, always ask which is most important and do that first.
- **Get results.** Do your work efficiently, accurately, and punctually.
- **Be a problem solver not a problem maker.** Every workplace offers the opportunity to problem solve, yet many people simply don't offer suggestions or solutions that could solve the problems. Look for opportunities in which you can make suggestions that will benefit the company. You shine when you help your company do something differently or more efficiently and it results in making more money, saving time, or reducing expenses. Those are the contributions that bosses and upper management never forget. When a problem arises, talk to your boss. Be concise, clearly state the problem, and offer a couple of possible solutions. Ask what the boss wants you to do. Even if you disagree with the boss's solution, acknowledge and accept it, implement it, and move on.
- **If your goal is to move ahead, identify the key players that control your internal future (your boss, your manager's boss, the HR director, and so on).** Now outline a plan of action.

- **Define what actions and/or behavior changes you need to make to improve your relationship with your supervisor.**

- **Consider having a career development or professional development meeting with your boss, and if it's okay, include her boss, as well.** Do this annually.

- **Develop a relationship with someone in HR to learn about internal openings, and to determine if you'll need more training to move up in this organization.**

- **Relocation is a necessary evil for many people trying to move ahead.** If you are employed in a large organization you may find yourself contemplating a relocation offer. Think long and hard before you say no. No matter how it's presented, a no answer will generally plateau your career with that company. Weigh the pros and cons of the family impact, and if you're married consider your spouse's career. Define your feelings about accepting a promotion and relocation, and where you will and will not go.

- **Stay in touch with previous managers.** As your boss moves on, you might be able to move on and up. When she leaves the company, get a written letter of recommendation, a new home email and phone numbers. Try to remember her with a Christmas card, occasional email or phone call. Treat these references like pure gold. They are. They can tell you about new jobs and be the reference that clinches your landing a new position. Reconnecting is simply a smart career move.

In summary, you are best served by creating a good working relationship with your boss. You do best if you are clear on the boss's goals and focus on achieving her priorities. It's wise to ask for that manager's counsel on your professional development. New skills, developed strengths, and achieving results will better ensure your success and future.

> *The will to win, the desire to succeed, the urge to reach your full potential . . . these are the keys that will unlock the door to personal excellence.*

EDDIE ROBINSON,
college football's "winningest" coach

CHAPTER 12

BUILD A POWER NETWORK

No matter how great *Brand You* is, if no one knows about it you'll face a difficult time advancing your career. An important strategic move is to expand your personal network and *actively* grow and nurture it over your professional lifetime. You should strive to make contacts with the specific purpose of letting others know who you are, what you do, and how you can be a resource to them, and to establish a positive frame of reference in their minds concerning you and your talents.

Most people realize networking is very important when they are job hunting. In fact, Department of Labor statistics say that two thirds of all jobs last year were found through personal or business contacts. Many job hunters actively develop their professional network as they search for a new position. For many, though, networking takes a backseat 98% of the time while they are employed in the new job. Talking to strangers is, of course, easier for an extroverted person than an introverted one, but no matter what your level of social comfort is, you need to develop and maintain a career network over the course of your working lifetime. An important function of your network is the help people in it can provide. Your contacts can advise you, make recommendations, assist you in solving conflicts, help you explore new projects, and be supports or mentors in your current position. A good professional network is especially valuable for bouncing around ideas and problem solving.

The wise, career-savvy *Brand You* intuitively knows it is important to cultivate contacts throughout her entire career. Yet most never methodically do this. You must nurture long-term professional relationships, establish contacts in business associations, and internally with coworkers, managers, clients, customers, and even service providers or vendors.

Lee was a business analyst for FedEx. He was a quiet, introverted, and analytical man who found networking tremendously difficult. Yet when he wanted to obtain a promotion outside his current division, I recommended he begin strategically networking. The first step was to visit the company HR director and ask for her assistance. He met her several times to discuss his career and goals, and after a few visits, she began to be more open and helpful. She gave him the name of the potential boss for the position he was interested in pursuing. He emailed the manager and asked for an appointment. The meeting went well and they informally discussed the job opportunity. Lee got some valuable insights.

Lee told that manager he would be applying for the job, which would be a promotion for him. He continued to ask for referrals and found two people who worked in the new department and contacted them. After he obtained additional information on the job, and a new ally, he created a targeted cover letter and resumé, defining *Brand Lee* and the valuable contributions he believed he'd be able to make in the new position. His new ally gave him some ideas on handling the interview, and he landed the coveted position. His internal networking was very helpful in his landing this promotion.

JOB SEARCH NETWORKING

I RECENTLY HAD a long conversation with some HR managers, discussing *Brand You* and job hunting. Denise, a *Fortune* 100 HR director of recruiting noted that 63% of all jobs are found through contacts. She added, "Referrals from colleagues and employers are fostered because we often get our best hires that way. An employer is looking for someone who knows something about the job and who can understand the specific skills needed. Often our contacts can recommend someone who would do a good job for us. We listen to our contacts because they have their fingers on the pulse of those with a good reputation in the marketplace. After all, interviewers are often just looking at a resumé, or they may be talking to a reference on the phone. It's hard to know who will do the job exceptionally well. That's why I think this idea of developing a favorable personal brand reputation that others recognize is exactly the kind of thing an employee or potential job candidate really needs to do to distinguish himself or herself. We hire for specific achievement and talents. We hire people who get results. Few candidates clearly promote who they are, what they are capable of doing, and the skills they have that are superior to those of the competition. A referral builds our confidence that the candidate can do the job."

COMMONALITY IS A KEY

AN OUTSIDE INTEREST can be the means for developing a professional connection. Golfing, hiking, boating, working out, neighborhood parties, or any other activity can lead to making new contacts. Many business deals, promotions, and new jobs have been secured walking around the golf course.

Patty met Ellen, a high-level manager, quite by accident while pursing her hobby. They both enjoyed scrapbooking and each often joined a group of women who showed up at a crafts store on Friday nights to create memory books. Neither liked to go alone and soon they were setting up more scrapbooking dates together. Over time, Ellen became a mentor to Patty as they sat and put family pictures in their scrapbooks, offering valuable career advice to Patty.

Working parents can expand their network by socializing with the parents of their kids' friends. Sporting events, school functions, committees, play groups—the possibilities are endless for meeting other parents who can become part of your informal network. Be genuinely friendly and at some point learn what kind of work they do and where they work. You never know when a casual acquaintance will be the contact you need.

An often overlooked but incredible resource for networking is connecting with your college alumni association. You'll find a goldmine of contacts because schools now have extensive networking systems and clubs that allow you to easily locate fellow graduates who live in or work at a place that you'd like to be. The school is your connection. This network can help you find a new job, get a promotion, or secure new clients or customers. Contact your alumni association to learn about how you can meet some folks who can positively impact your career.

NETWORKING DOS AND DON'TS

Dos

- Take the initiative at a meeting or gathering to introduce yourself.
- Learn a person's first name, shake hands, and make eye contact during the conversation.
- Learn to make small talk to be able to start and maintain conversations.
- Look for a connection such as a hobby, sport, hometown, college, or school.
- Be active in introducing people to each other and comment on any common link they might have.
- Have a sentence or two prepared that describes *Brand You* in a concise but friendly way.
- If you want a referral, don't beat around the bush, simply ask for it.
- Listen attentively to others and be genuinely interested.
- Keep in touch. An occasional phone call now and then is much more memorable than an email.
- Offer to be a resource to others.
- Invite someone you want to get to know to a party, dinner, or event you are hosting or attending.
- Send a handwritten thank-you note when appropriate.
- Reciprocate. Do a favor for a favor.
- Respect a person's time by making any networking informational interview brief, no more than fifteen or twenty minutes.

Don'ts

- Don't be a pest; once you cross the line, it is hard to recover.
- Don't exclude people from your network efforts. Everyone has connections in both low and high places.

- Don't be presumptuous and do respect the time and situation of another when you make a request.
- Do not ask, ask, ask, and then never give reciprocal information.
- Don't try to name drop or impress someone new.
- Don't play the one-upmanship game—it does not make friends or influence people.
- Don't monopolize the conversation.
- Don't overdrink—it will not make you more social and could send out a message that you have a problem.

MAKE NETWORKING A KEY
LONG-TERM TACTIC

NETWORKING IS A lifelong process, important not just for the few months you spend looking for a job. The Department of Labor surveys state that two-thirds of all new jobs were found through contacts and networking. Many people are aware of this labor market statistic but few know that it has been nearly constant for more than a decade. Your job hunting network is a key strategy to finding new work. You often scramble to make contacts when you unexpectedly become unemployed. It takes a great deal of energy to reestablish contacts if you only use them when you need them. You're better off maintaining an ongoing network of former bosses, coworkers, friends, and acquaintances over time so that when you do need them, they are all ready to help you.

Networking is also a key strategy in learning how to improve on the job. Getting to know other people who may hold the same job title as you allows you to share information and ideas, as well as problem solve together. This becomes very important if you're in a management or professional position because oftentimes you may be working alone at your company and may not have a lot of peers readily available. It's important to join associations and professional groups. Make an extra effort when you attend conferences or workshops to make some new professional friends. Through email or a quick phone call you can develop a friendship that benefits you and your contacts. Ask for their insight, recommendations, or guidance and anything you think they might find useful. By creating those relationships, you'll find that improving at your job becomes a great deal easier.

One key strategy is to expand your network and get to know others with power and influence. That often seems easier if you've moved up the ladder and are more senior in your career. It can seem like mission impossible, however, when you are just starting out. Be on the lookout for connections through family, friends, alumni contacts, or people who have already developed a great brand in your field. You might want to identify and ask someone who can be a mentor to you. Don't be misled by the old-fashioned concept that he'll take you under his wing, protect you, and keep you from making any mistakes on the job. That is simply a myth. But a mentor can help you understand office politics, introduce you to key players, get you involved with more important management projects, and be a good person to learn from. Joining an association or professional group is a great way to find and learn from a mentor.

As you build your career, you will have an easier time if you realize that you must become a lifetime networker.

List ten specific ways to build your network over the next year.
  1.
  2.
  3.
  4.
  5.
  6.
  7.
  8.
  9.
 10.

List five people you'd like to meet and develop relationships with.

1.

2.

3.

4.

5.

THE ALL-IMPORTANT CAREER IDENTITY CARD

PEOPLE NEED TO be able to easily remember you. Offering your business card, even if it's one you have created, is a terrific idea. It's a way to quickly give others your contact information in order to cement a new relationship. A business card is something you can create for yourself. These are quite easy to make with any computer these days. We created the following examples using a $29 graphics software program called Printmaster. There are many other software programs you can use, or go online and order business cards from an office supply website such as Office Depot or Staples. Include your name, address, home or cell phone number, and home email (if you are not using your work contact information). Do use a job title and any unique areas of specialty you want to emphasize.

Your business card allows for easier networking. It identifies who you are and it is an essential business tool. Never leave home without yours. The following business card examples tell us who the person is, his contact info, and what he does.

Additionally, along with your written business cards you need a verbal business card, which is a memorized introduction designed to allow another person to quickly understand who you are and what you are good at. An abbreviated *Brand You*, if you will. It certainly isn't all of your background, nor is it a lengthy autobiography. Just create two or three sentences that give the other person a memorable overview of you and your level of ability.

Ken Slone
19 Mill Street
Seton Hall, NJ
01356
781.555.9987
Kenslone89@aol.com

PARALEGAL

Here are four different examples of what a networker might say if he went to a professional conference attended by individuals from various backgrounds and fields.

Ken could use this approach to make a change and get promoted:

"Hi I'm Ken Stone. I've been a personal injury paralegal for a large law firm for the last ten years. I'm also the vice president of our state paralegal association. Currently I'm seeking to move into an administrator position. I've just completed my business degree in management."

Linda is just looking to expand her network; she might use this kind of an introduction:

FINANCIAL ANALYST
BUDGETS ■ FORECASTING ■ MODELING

Linda Davidson, MBA

1234 House Avenue
Scarsdale, NY 13345
Phone: (315)555-7890
Cell: (351)555-1000
E-mail: lindavidson@hotmail.com

"Nice to meet you, I'm Linda Davidson, a *Fortune* 500 financial analyst, with an MBA from NYU. I work mostly on projecting future sales revenues, and establishing annual budgets. What do you do?"

Brenda had few professional friends and, hoping to make one or two, she might use this approach:

"Hello, I'm Brenda Capestany. I'm an ESL teacher who specializes in helping Latinos quickly learn the English language so they can gain employment. I was born in Mexico City and moved to the United States in my secondary school years and went to college at Cal State, San Bernardino."

BRENDA CAPESTANY

ESL TEACHER BILINGUAL IN SPANISH & ENGLISH

12340 NE 212TH STREET
ORANGE, CA 99100
PHONE 714-456-7890
E-MAIL BCAPESTANY@MSN.COM

Julia created a card for herself after being a stay-at-home mom for six years. She's now trying to reenter the workforce. She could introduce herself this way:

"I'm looking to begin another phase of my life in fundraising. I've been involved in planning school auctions, galas, and other special events, and find I have quite the knack for that. I'd like to work for a nonprofit or school as I feel very strongly about the importance of quality education, and that's a mission I'd like to continue to support."

Each person offered a few facts in their introduction, but left the conversation open to find some common ground of interest. Maybe it's the degree you have, the college you went to,

Julia Toile
Fundraiser

—auctions
—special events
—galas

4 Simms Street
St. Louis, MO 64345
818.555.3526
Jtoile@att.net

or your hometown. It might be the specialty or the job you do. A rehearsed introduction can make it easier for you to get a conversation started when you attend a conference and meet new people.

STRATEGIC VOLUNTEERING TO ADVANCE
BRAND YOU

YOU MUST BE visible. *Brand You* cannot survive or flourish in a vacuum. That means taking the initiative but being very selective about what you'll get from the volunteer effort.

Use volunteering to acquire a new skill or perfect an old one. Many people join Toastmasters to practice the art of public speaking. Others take on a leadership role in the local Rotary Club or in a professional association to gain visibility and get some management experience. One woman wanted to be a writer and editor but lacked formal experience. She volunteered at her church and did the school and parish newsletter. It was well done, quite creative, and got her recruited for a real job paying a nice salary as a newsletter editor. Many people have acquired conference planning skills by organizing professional events. Whatever skill you want to hone, there is likely to be a volunteer activity to learn and use it in.

Barbara was a hard worker, quiet and dependable. She really wanted to get into management. She'd graduated from college but was still working in an insurance company staff position. She had hoped that once she completed her long-sought-after bachelor's degree, her promotion would be a shoe in. It wasn't so. During our counseling session, Barbara realized that she had indeed been confined to a very small department in a company of thousands of employees. Her assignments to advance *Brand Barbara* were as follows:

1. Go down to HR and set up an appointment to ask them how she might better position herself to move ahead. She would need to establish a relationship with the HR manager so that person knew her and would recognize her in the future. This took a few visits, and she got some good leads from developing this relationship.
2. Ask her boss for some career assistance and guidance to move ahead.
3. Contact other department managers and set appointments up with them.
4. Network internally making her strengths and goals known.
5. Join the budget planning group or computer system group to expand her company contacts.

Her efforts paid off and she moved into the management ranks.

You can expand your network if you volunteer to work on committees, causes, political events, community service projects, and so on. Since your free time is precious, give thought to exactly how you can advance your skills and get yourself better known among your peers or coworkers. Strategic volunteering is the fastest route. The two forms of strategic volunteering are as follows:

- Internal—volunteering for projects important to top or upper management. Don't choose the company picnic, but planning committees, new important projects, writing part of the company's annual report, and so on.
- External—volunteering for associations, service organizations, political groups, and professional trade positions. Any role that can aid you in moving ahead.

MENTORS AND EXPERTS

LEARN FROM THE best. Books and articles often are goldmines for learning. When you need a bit of detailed information ask those you know if they can introduce you to an expert in the field. Or check the Web for an author who is knowledgeable on the subject. Oftentimes an email to one of these contacts can get you a wealth of top-notch information. For those more established in their careers, these brief encounters with high level executives or experts can lead to further mentoring sessions.

Someone early in their career should think about finding a mentor—or two or three. You don't need to learn all things from one person. You can contact different people for different areas of assistance and guidance. No one is going to always pave the path for you. But a caring mentor can help you avoid political battles, resolve personality issues, advise on promotions, and solve logistical problems. Typically, a mentor is more experienced than you are, thrives on fostering other people's successes, and is a confidant or sounding board. Sometimes your boss or another manger can fit the bill perfectly. Other times you need to look to associations or committees to find an ideal mentor.

An ongoing mentor relationship is a two-way street. It needs to benefit both people and be a reciprocal situation. You can share your goals and ask your mentor to help you network more frequently and better establish *Brand You*. Above all, if you have a mentor you need to be sincere and genuine in showing appreciation and respect for his time and attention. The mentor typically enjoys sharing knowledge but wants to be appreciated, too.

In today's ever-changing workplace, where people come and go quickly, you are more likely to find mini-mentors along the way. These are people who offer some guidance here or there, more informally than you might wish. Take guidance from whomever you can—a speaker at a conference, an author of an important trade article, the CEO's secretary, your neighbor—any person who willingly aids your career. Suppose you needed to learn a new software application. You could take a one-day crash course but you'd also benefit by finding an internal expert—a secretary or a systems guy—to use as a resource and learn from.

Some people select a mentor they have never met. They subscribe to newsletters and read educational materials and books to learn from an authority. Just because you aren't conversing directly doesn't mean you can't be inspired and develop new ideas by learning from others. Any method that helps you improve—tapes, books, articles, chats, discussion lists, e-newsletters, and so on—all mentor you to advance and become better than you are currently.

In summary, make networking a vital and deliberate part of your career management strategy. Through work, play, and social contacts, you meet others and cultivate relationships that help you gain new knowledge, advice, and yet more contacts when you need them. Being a resource to others is the best way to become a terrific networker. For as you help others, others will willingly help you.

> *It doesn't matter who you are, or where you come from. The ability to triumph always begins with you.*
>
> **OPRAH WINFREY**

CHAPTER 13

COMMUNICATE *BRAND YOU*

esumés, cover letters, references, interview skills, and email writing are essential navigational tools in your professional life. Learning to articulate your career identity concisely so *Brand You* is easy to recognize is a key part of this toolbox.

The fastest way to get hired or promoted is to be enthusiastically recommended by someone that the decision maker respects. Even a reference from a former boss that isn't known can greatly influence employers when considering promotions or job offers. Having your contacts send on your resume to hiring managers is the best way to be assured you'll be looked upon as a solid candidate for any job opening.

YOUR RESUMÉ

CREATE A STELLAR resumé. Employers hate fluff. They want a customized resumé that specifically addresses your qualifications for the stated job needs. Over the past few years, poor or embarrassing hiring mistakes have made employers much more thorough, cautious, and even suspicious when hiring for open positions.

Hiring the wrong person is very costly in dollars and productivity losses. When an employer glances through dozens, if not hundreds, of resumés, he seeks the few that stand out. Your resumé must clearly illustrate *Brand You* and be easily and quickly absorbed. It should be clear and concise and define your accomplishments. And it must be accurate! Think Actions = Results, a formula to keep in mind when you sit down to develop your resumé. Whether you are job hunting, or going after an internal opening, your resumé must be top notch. Taking the time to create a terrific resumé, one that establishes your career identity quickly and succinctly, is imperative.

Let's help you determine if your resumé clearly and concisely outlines *Brand You* and makes you stand out in the crowd by completing the test below.

The Stand-Out-in-a-Crowd Resumé Quiz

Is your resumé one page and targeted to a specific job?

Tip: Employers scan resumés with a fifteen-to-twenty-second glance. Be a skillful editor, deleting the portions that are irrelevant or least helpful to your securing a particular position. Today's employers want one page only. Emphasize your experience in the last five to seven years. Use different resumés to target different job titles so that each resumé fully outlines the abilities and accomplishments that are relevant to performing the job. Specifics sell; generalizations and boring job descriptions without lists of results do not.

Does your resumé describe results and accomplishments?

Tip: Employers want proof that you can achieve results. They look at your future potential by noting what you've accomplished to date. Specifics that demonstrate your accomplishments are crucial. Use descriptive terms to indicate how you saved money, or time, made money or contributed to productivity and the bottom line. Use specific percentages and figures.

Is your resumé visually appealing?

Tip: The importance of the appearance of your printed resumé cannot be overemphasized! Use high-quality paper. Watch spacing and margins. Allow for lots of white space and margins. Make use of italics, capitals, underlining, bolding, indentations, and bullets to emphasize your important points. Use a computer and get a laser printed copy of your resumé to give it a sharp, professional look. Be sure your name, phone number, and email are large enough to be easily seen. Proofread—make your resumé a perfect example of you!

Does your resumé include a summary of qualifications section?

Tip: This five-to-six-sentence section should emphasize your brand. It summarizes your experience and top selling points to do the job.

Do you know the rules on using an electronic resumé?

Tip: When emailing or posting a resumé always be sure the document is created in MS word. Many employers complain that people send resumés from home systems created in Works and the employer gets a file of unreadable code when he opens it. Keywords and various job titles are essential in the electronic resumé as many of these resumés get scanned and sorted by a computer. Be careful to not use any decorative lines. Keep fonts simple.

Can your faxed resumé be easily read?

Tip: Fax it to a friend. Be sure that the type is easy to read, your phone number is clearly legible; and it's printed dark enough to be easily read (but not so dark that words blur), as faxing can distort. Use font size twelve or higher in a clean font like Arial.

Are you starting each sentence with an action verb?

Tip: Begin sentences with descriptive action verbs such as established, analyzed, implemented, designed, organized. They add power to your sentences. Never start any sentence in a resumé with the word "I."

Is your tone positive, without personal statistics and abbreviations?

Tip: Spell out names of schools, cities, and abbreviations completely. It is more professional to give complete information, as employers may not recognize abbreviations or acronyms. Never state why you left a position or previous salary. It is no longer considered professional or wise to include information about marital status, gender, height, weight, or health or a picture on your resumé.

Does your resumé get you interviews that are an appropriate fit?

Tip: This crucial factor lets you know that written your brand is being recognized by employers. If you are not getting interviews, or you are getting inappropriate ones, it's time to seriously revise your resumé, emphasizing Actions = Results.

Every year, update your resumé, and keep a current version on hand that you can use if something interesting comes up.

Let the tips listed above be your guide on how your resumé must look to compete in today's workplace.

The current HR mantra seems to be, "There are indeed a lot of poor candidate choices out there." These professionals complain that their in-boxes have turned into resumé junk piles and that they receive too many resumés from unqualified people. Don't allow your resumé to be lost in the heap. Define *Brand You* in a targeted, specific, results-oriented resumé. (For more help, consult my book *Winning Resumes,* available at www.RobinRyan.com.)

PERFORMANCE APPRAISALS

AT PERFORMANCE APPRAISAL time, bring an updated resumé to the meeting. During the twelve months prior to your appraisal, keep a monthly log of all your duties. Note any new tasks you have taken on and state accomplishments, special projects, and any recognition you have received, and present those at your review. They can make a positive impact. Your organization may ask you to rate yourself. Your annual log makes this easier to do. Take credit for your accomplishments. Ask for more work in areas in which you excel. Discuss your goals, your strengths, and your concerns. Be sure to include any important new skills or accomplishments that merit extra consideration for a more significant raise or promotion. Save your review. It's a valuable endorser of *Brand You*, particularly if it's a good one. You never know when you might need to use it.

COVER LETTERS

IT'S AMAZING HOW so many people tell me that they that hate to write cover letters. That is not good, since employers LOVE them. The results of a national hiring survey published in my book *Winning Cover Letters*, showed that cover letters were *very influential*.

The cover letter is the first introduction of *Brand You* to an employer. The letter is often viewed as a measuring stick on how good your communication skills are. Take your time to skillfully create and review any cover letter you sign your name to. The trick is to use an opening paragraph that attracts attention. Ninety-six percent of hiring managers surveyed like seeing a summary of experience and *Brand You* distinguished right up front in your opening paragraph.

My client Elizabeth applied online for a position as facilities director. She included this cover letter with her resumé, even though only a resumé was requested, and got a successful interview. See how clearly her brand stands out in this example.

Elizabeth O'Hara, PE
121 Clover Street, Rochester, NY 13442
716.555.6125
elizohara@aol.com

Joe Northrup, HR Director
City of Rochester
105 Main Street
Rochester NY 13445

Re: Facilities Director

Dear Joe:

With twenty years experience in Facilities and Project Management, I'd bring award-winning leadership and proven budget and resource management expertise to your facilities director position. Highlights of my background include:

- Directed the regional public works and facilities operations for multiple locations with $200-million annual budget, receiving Outstanding Job Performance Awards.
- Manager of facilities, effectively handling planning, resource allocation, budgets, scheduling, logistics, team development and supervision, environmental impacts, space allocation, capital improvements, and ongoing project management.
- Served as project manager on a $67-million new construction facility, delivering this facility on time and under budget.
- Extensive experience planning for space needs that improved facilities and resource uses.
- Recognized in past positions for building highly productive teams.

I'd like to discuss in greater detail the valuable benefits I could bring to Rochester's Public Works team. I can be reached at 716.555.6125.

Your time and consideration is most appreciated.

Sincerely,

Elizabeth O'Hara

Although she received an email confirmation, I encouraged Elizabeth to actually mail a hard copy of her cover letter and resumé to the city HR director. It is a wise strategy to do both since electronic submissions don't always work and auto replies deceive you into thinking they have. Hundreds of job seekers had applied for this position, and when she went in for an interview, Elizabeth learned it was the postal copy they had in hand. She was well prepared and thrilled when, a week later, she landed this job, negotiating a very nice salary, too.

Test your cover letter savvy by taking the Cover Letter Quiz at www.RobinRyan.com/tools.

EMAIL

EMAIL IS THE way people communicate inside many companies today. A smart strategy to implement and *always* utilize is to spell-check before you click *send*. This will alert you to any typos. An email full of misspelled words will make you look less intelligent or just plain careless.

Carefully compose your thoughts and review everything before clicking *send*. You must always keep *Brand You* in mind when you sit at the keyboard. Emailing jokes (especially anything sexual), deep confessions, flirtations, flame mail, or conspiracies and the like, can be tracked by your boss or those in upper management. Big Brother occasionally does email audits. It's wise to keep work email strictly business. Flame mail might make you notorious, but is viewed as a *big* negative to higher-ups. Be professional—others are watching.

INTERVIEWS

INEVITABLY, IN YOUR quest to manage your career and reach your goals, you'll have a job or promotion interview. You must establish *Brand You* quickly. Your ability to say you are great will be 100% stronger if you give clear examples that paint a picture of how you've accomplished your work tasks in the past. So instead of answering questions in vague or generic terms, tell a story by giving a past example that illustrates the results or use of a skill.

You might find taking the *Interactive Interview Readiness Quiz* advantageous before you enter your next interview. Go to www.RobinRyan.com /tools to take the test.

A great illustration of how *Brand You* influences hiring managers was demonstrated by Janelle's experience when she applied for a technical designer position. She had interviews with Saks five times, never landing the designer job. Although her qualifications were strong, a year after her relocation to New York, she was still unemployed. She sought help. In our counseling session we worked on defining and better projecting *Brand Janelle*.

First we zeroed in on her top five selling points. I taught her how to create a verbal business card, aka the 60 Second Sell™, in which she links her top selling points into a few sentences that summarize *Brand Janelle*. We then worked on answering questions. She was a reserved and analytical person and had to work hard to be able to answer questions so her career identity came though. It did the trick; she received two job offers just days apart, electing to join Saks.

Before you go to your next interview, look over these interview success guidelines:

- Conduct research on the company and specifics of the job beforehand.
- Write out and practice answering potential questions.
- Prepare and focus your mind, attitude, and conversation on success and effectively communicating your ability to do the employer's job.
- Know what your most appealing talents and top selling points are.
- Ask impressive questions.
- Learn salary negotiation techniques.

In summary, your career toolbox must contain a current, attention-getting, and effective resumé; targeted cover letters; first-class references; good interview skills; and email-writing expertise. These are essential to every career transition and all must be aligned with promoting *Brand You*.

PART 5

CREATING
YOUR FUTURE DESTINY

> " Carpe diem, quam minimum credula postero. "
> *(Seize the day, put no trust in tomorrow.)*

HORACE,
poet

CHAPTER 14

BRAND YOU ACTION PLAN

uccess is no accident.

American speed skater Dan Jansen competed at the 1988 Olympic Games and was the heavy favorite to take home the gold medal. On the very day he was to compete, his sister, Jane, died from leukemia. Determined, he took to the ice but fell rounding a turn and was eliminated. He went home without a medal.

Four more years of training and dreaming brought Jansen to the 1992 Olympic Games. He was the defending World Cup champion in the 500-meter and was predicted to be an Olympic winner. Jansen's one minor stumble was enough to keep him off the medal podium. He finished in fourth place, *thirty-two hundredths of a second behind* the bronze medal winner.

In the 1994 games, older and at the end of his Olympic skating career, he went out for one last try. Many thought he was too far past his prime to bring home a medal. As the 500-meter race began, Jansen lost his balance coming around a turn, dragged his hand on the ice, and came in eighth. The 1,000-meter was his final race, and it was a distance that—by his own admission—wasn't his forte. Jansen took off like gangbusters, and by the 800-meter mark was on a world-record pace. When he staggered yet again, the whole world gasped. But this time, he was able to right himself. Dan Jansen crossed the finish line in 1:12:43, winning his first and only gold medal, setting a new world record to boot. The entire world stood up and cheered.

Oh, boy, did they cheer! I can still recall seeing Dan skating around the rink in his victory celebration, carrying his baby daughter in his arms, in front of ten thousand screaming live fans and millions of thrilled Americans who watched his incredible victory on television.

You will probably never compete for an Olympic gold medal. I know I won't. But we sure can learn a lot about the drive and determination that a person like Dan Jansen used to take home his gold medal. Jansen knew that believing in yourself, being steadfast and determined, and doing your best while concentrating on achieving your goal can really make any dream come true.

Success. Achievement. Ambition. Goals. Dreams. Happiness. Power. Victory. Recognition. Awards. So many single words convey a reward that only you yourself can define.

As you create your own future, you need to examine your heart and answer these important questions.

What is your ambition?
What does success mean to you?
How will you know, specifically, when you've achieved it?
What is the level of effort you are willing to put out to achieve it?

Dan Jansen certainly knew his ambition, his goal, and what success would look like. As you develop *Brand You*, you do need to have a clear focus on your goals, your dreams, and ambition.

Your goals for success are set by you. They matter to you. The world needs excellence in so many jobs that you can find your favorite and be the best possible at it. You may want to be a terrific French chef, a dedicated nurse, a teacher who inspires others to learn about history or culture, an actuary, a programmer, a manager. There are thousands of jobs and special niches out there you can cultivate into your dream position.

Our careers develop in stages and our interests, objectives, and goals change as we mature. In the early stage of our career the goal is to focus on learning, acquiring some skills and professional experience, and achieving good results. The attitude at this stage is one of enthusiasm to charge forward and be promoted. In midcareer a person may switch priorities to allow more family time, or fast-forward to land bigger promotions and make more money. At fifty, career goals may shift again, often coming with a personal transformation and an emphasis on fulfilling long-held desires. People look to the future and realize that they want to leave a legacy behind. Others just want an easier, less stressful, or part-time job, so they have more leisure time.

Brand You is about creating a successful attitude and clearly defining the genius inside. You, too, can reach the highest levels of success and achievement and attain any dream that you set for yourself.

THE SKY CAN BE THE LIMIT— SO I ALWAYS SAY DREAM BIG!

FOR ONE CLIENT this meant starting a school, for another, heading the international division. Another wanted to make the same salary, working part-time. But Alex had a different dream. I'm telling his story because the road to great success often has twists, turns, and challenges to overcome.

Alex had plenty of determination. He was an engineer for a large manufacturer, had been there a few years, and rated his job just okay. He dreamed of a career as a day trader. Day trading is a risky field, with no school or classes available, and Alex learned on the job the hard way. He began trading after work and lost his $50,000 savings. Determined that he would succeed, Alex took a lien on his house and maxed out his credit cards. He lost all that money, too. He admits that he made a lot of mistakes, but he felt that if he kept studying the market, he would succeed. He withdrew his 401K, but he quickly lost that, too. He was down to his final $2,500. At age twenty-nine, having lost more than $100,000, he faced the monumental decision to stay with a secure engineering job or pursue the day trading career. Deciding to go with his passion, he finally found his groove and slowly regained all the money he had lost. Now, three years later, Alex is a very successful and secure day trader.

Alex's key to success was using his innate talents. He's a risk taker, very self-directed, a loner, not a team player. Analytical and methodical, he thrived in a fast-changing environment. His strong self-discipline, ability to make quick decisions, and a single focus and drive are the perfect qualifications for the job he chose.

Few thirty-two-year-olds live in a two-million-dollar house and command an annual income of $750,000 as Alex now does. "I've always been successful at everything I've put my mind to," Alex told me. "While I call it drive, my wife says it's obsession. Whatever you call it, for me, not succeeding was simply not an option. I'm very goal driven and have confidence in my own abilities. My advice to others is to rely just on your talents and use them daily in your job. It has to be a job that you are passionate about. I can't wait to wake up every day and surround myself in the excitement of the stock market and day trading. My final tip is this: believe in yourself. I had a dream to make it as a day trader. I worked hard, found a mentor, and spent hours studying and researching on my own. When everyone told me to get out and quit, I refused to listen. It's pretty scary to be down to $2,500 knowing you've lost $100,000. I was no rich kid playing around. I scrimped and saved that money. I viewed failures as my education and normal fare on the road to success. Now I'm loving every day of my job and plan to use my talents every day of my life."

That's passion! Although day trading and the risks Alex took are not for most of us, he is living the life of his dreams. Living the life of your dreams is the goal I've set for you. Consider these revealing questions to move in this direction:

- What do I still want to achieve?
- What makes me come alive and get excited?
- What is my driving passion and motivation?

Suzanne Willis Zoglio, author of *Create a Life That Tickles Your Soul* stated, "There is no such thing as standing still. According to the laws of physics, living systems either grow or they begin to break down. This is true of the mind, body, and spirit. To seize growth opportunities we must move out of our comfort zones. And that takes courage and discipline."

You, too, can change your life and achieve whatever you can dream if only you put in the effort and determination.

Negative, self-sabotaging internal talk is the enemy that most often derails people's lives and their careers. Insecurity and low self-esteem can be addressed head-on by implementing a program for change. Using written strategies that improve your attitude, increase your pride, and build your sense of self-worth and personal affirmation, must be implemented.

"Every negative thing you think, say, or do damages your spirit and keeps you from flying, as it affects you mentally, physically, and spiritually. Everyone has gifts and talents that are special and unique to them. You must let yours come out," writes Dottie Billington, author of *Life Is an Attitude*.

Life changes you. Companies change; some great ones can

become dysfunctional, especially during hard times, during and after a merger, or because upper management allows it. Almost overnight, a new boss can reshape a happy workplace into a nightmare of new demands and personality conflicts. Monitor your organization's attitude. If your company or department is a place you dread going to, you should move on. There are always new employers who offer incredible places to grow and flourish.

BRAND YOU IS G.R.E.A.T.

SO WHAT DOES being G.R.E.A.T. mean? It means being happy and successful in whatever you choose for your life's work. It is also the acronym of your formula to define *Brand You* and achieve your objectives and desires. Here is what it stands for:

G—Goals
R—Results
E—Excellence
A—Actions and Attitudes
T—Team Standout

To be G.R.E.A.T. (or G.R.E.A.T.er), you set goals. You achieve results. You excel in using your talents and doing your job. You implement actions and put forth a "can-do-will-do-done attitude, which will make you visible, memorable, and a team or company standout.

With a plan, you can conquer the world. You need to be a man or a woman with a plan!

The most successful people in the world envision their next success. They have written goals with action steps noted to achieve them. Only 3% of the population put their goals in writing. Yet outcomes are typically achieved 20% faster with written goals according to behavioral psychologists.

The most common reason most workers don't set goals is that they haven't been taught how. Those who have learned often opt for the lazy approach and never sit down to lay the action plan out in writing. A goal that is not in writing is merely a fantasy. It has no practical energy behind it. Goal setting is work, and some serious self-assessment is required. Many people have such a fear of failure that they operate on the standby of, "If you don't have goals, you can't fail." There are still others, particularly women, who devalue themselves from a fear of success. Then there are the folks who are unwilling to make the sacrifice or pay the price to achieve their goals. You won't be a doctor if you skip going to medical school. You must believe you can achieve it and be willing to work for it or you simply sabotage yourself and do not succeed.

S.M.A.R.T. goals is a savvy but simple tool for goal setting to establish your goals with an action plan in place to achieve them. The formula is:

Specific—a written goal with all steps necessary to complete it.

Measurable—you and others can see how you are progressing.

Achievable—stretching but doable.

Realistic—relying only on your own efforts.

Targeted—a clear objective noting consequences and potential rewards.

Dream BIG! Your future is whatever you make it. Read your goals daily and as you achieve them, replace them with new dreams to keep your life interesting and yourself motivated to achieve whatever you want.

Many people get stuck trying to define their goals. If this is you, get moving in the right direction. Work with a coach, read some insightful and directive books, or attend a goal-setting and time-management seminar.

ACTION STEP—
ACHIEVING SUCCESSFUL OUTCOMES

DO NOT THINK that goals and outcomes are the same. Goals are conceptual. Outcomes are what actually happens. We must set goals and outline exactly how we'll get the desired results.

- Decide on and write down exactly what you want or need to live the life you dream about in your career and in your personal life. This is your ultimate goal.
- Outline, step by step, everything you need to do to achieve this goal.
- Write down some interim goals, clearly and concisely. Make them specific and measurable. Break these goals into doable pieces. List the action steps necessary to achieve them.
- Note desirable outcomes that are reasonable and achievable.
- Organize your list into a detailed plan.
- Act on your plan immediately. Do something to get started.
- Resolve to do something that moves you forward every day
- Set deadlines.
- Define problems or obstacles you are likely to encounter and list people, books, or resources that can help you overcome these challenges.
- Visualize your success.

VISUALIZATIONS AND AFFIRMATIONS

IT'S YOUR RESPONSIBILITY to take control of your future. Through goal setting and creating action plans you can bypass derailments along your journey. Psychologists strongly encourage using these strategies to enrich your life, improve your self-esteem, influence life's outcomes. *Affirm* your willingness to embrace change and *visualize* the results.

Dr. Lynn Joseph, psychologist and author of *The Job Loss Recovery Guide,* says that if you consciously want to change, grow, and reach selected goals, your imagination is an indispensable tool. Use visualization or mental imaging, to foresee your more positive future. You can mentally rehearse that promotion interview, seeing yourself being effective and successful. It increases your personal power in stressful situations and can lead to a more positive and satisfying existence. Improve your vision of your own success.

- Befriend positive people that encourage and support you and have lofty goals of their own. They will inspire you. Tune out the naysayer or those who don't support your efforts.
- Stop being analytical all the time. Self-analysis often just looks at what's wrong. To dissect or criticize is great for looking at sales revenues but destructive when applied to individuals. It batters self-esteem. Whenever you begin to attack yourself, think, "How can I do this task?" instead of belaboring why you *can't* do it.
- Make self-talk positive. When the poisonous, negative, beat-you-up thoughts arise, drown them out with music. Play it loud—louder—so loud you cannot possibly hear anything negative.
- Acknowledge your gifts daily and reaffirm, out loud, at least five tasks or talents where you excel.
- Show a genuine interest in others. Help where you can. Acknowledge other people's success though compliments. Generously congratulate them by sending cards and notes. Not only does this make them feel good but it will develop positive relationships with others.
- Set realistic daily goals. Little bits and pieces you can achieve over time add up to great accomplishments.

- Exercise. You will feel better, think clearer, and be less stressed out. If you exercise at least four times each week, it will help you look better and feel better and be more productive.
- Drop the bad habits. Smoking, too much alcohol or food, or profanity bring you down.

The mental imaging technique does increase confidence. People need visual anchors for their goals. Some men have pictures pasted everywhere they look, especially pictures of the new luxury car or boat they plan to drive when they achieve their goals. Women often cut out articles or pictures of sunny beach locales, resort spas, or cruises ships, to remind them of what they'll get when they have achieved success. Others have a nice family photo illustrating a leisure activity they all enjoy. Visual anchors help you cement the goals. They turn on an internal cheerleader. These illustrations are constant reminders of your goals and they encourage you to mentally reaffirm who you are and how you plan to reach the ultimate goal—happiness.

A positive thought or idea that you consciously focus on to produce a desired result is a simple yet powerful tool. Affirmations, repeated to yourself, can transform your beliefs positively and powerfully.

Here's how to create useful affirmations to improve your life.

Write your affirmation, using the first person.

I _____

State it positively, as if were already true. Repeat it daily. Be very specific.

Here are some examples:

* I use my communication talents and strengths to bring the best into my life.
* I have overcome any obstacles that are blocking my career path.
* I've successfully completed the project and have been promoted because of the results I delivered.
* I have terrific organizational and planning skills and the boss praises me to his superiors.

Write out ten affirmations—positive statements about yourself—defining *why you are great*. Start each morning for the next thirty days repeating these out loud. They will become beliefs and influence your life in a more positive way.

1.

2.

3.

4.

5.

6.

7.

8.

9.

10.

You set your own dreams and your own actions, just as you have control and power over *Brand You.* You also control the choices you make. Elect to move forward with a solid, well-developed plan to obtain the life you want to live.

No one can do that for you, but you surely can do that for yourself! Carpe diem!

CHAPTER 15

BRAND YOU FOR A LIFETIME

our personal brand may change over your lifetime. Creating your career identity is a fluid thing. It is evolving; it changes. Our interests shift and our skills change, improve, or become archaic. We may have worked in an area that's now obsolete, or we've gotten too old to physically perform the work anymore. New technology comes in and sometimes, even though you're great at doing something, no one has a need for it any more. You need to pay attention to changing trends and project future needs.

Your innate, God-given talents do not change. You were born with these, which is why you must build your career, and any future direction you wish to take, on your strengths. Use them, adapt them, and think about what new position or field you want to pursue, and where you may wish to look, then go for it.

Developing and promoting *Brand You* is a resourceful way to be *sure* you are in the right place at the right time. When opportunity comes knocking, people will know who you are, and because you have branded yourself very well, they will recognize your potential and your value. You will use your natural talents in all you do throughout your life. Think transferable skills. If you are a good researcher, there will be many places to use that strength in your lifetime. These transferable skills are part of portable *Brand You*, and you'll use them wherever you land.

The career management approach outlined in this book can be summarized into these strategies:

- Build a career on your strengths, talents, and natural abilities; invest in your Brand Equity.
- Create core competencies that others recognize; develop your Brand Advantage.
- Work in a place where you are a good fit and your accomplishments are appreciated; discover your Brand Value.
- Develop a following in your chosen career; build a strong and admired Brand Reputation.
- Create a distinctive and sought-after Brand Image.
- Establish the genuine *Brand You*.

DO IT *NOW*!

ONE MOMENT IN time can change your life forever.

Kathryn was called into the CEO's office. It was a rare event and she felt a little nervous when she entered; both her boss and the CFO were there. Charles, the CEO, began, "Kathryn you've done a fantastic job here, particularly in forecasting sales revenues. Every one of us recognizes your contribution and talent so you're being promoted to director of finance. Congratulations!" He smiled warmly.

Dave, an IT supervisor who had a long career at the same company, strolled into the department meeting. He left with the shock of his life. The company would now be outsourcing the IT function, so Dave and his team were being laid off—effective immediately.

Michael had hoped against hope that a dream job in marketing would be his. When the phone rang, and it was the interviewer on the other end, he held his breath as self-doubt swept over him. The voice on the phone began slowly, saying, "Michael, we had several strong candidates. Your references spoke so highly of you that we feel lucky to have such a talented man want to join our team. The position is yours if you want it. We really hope you'll accept it."

Wow, in just seconds the unexpected, the unwanted, or even the dared-to-hope-for can change your life forever.

Of course, there are some really big life-altering events that change us all.

It was the babbling voices on the radio that woke me. My brain couldn't connect the words that the announcer was saying; it was something about explosions. The television's remote control was on the nightstand so I picked it up and quickly turned on the television. On CNN, Fox, and every other channel, the newscasters were describing the worst tragedy ever on American soil. Two airplanes had been flown into the World Trade Center towers and both had collapsed to the ground, taking the lives of thousands of people. I'd find out later that Billy, one of my college friends, lost his life that day. After that moment in time, no American would ever be the same.

We all have personal experiences that are life changing. It's the sudden, unexpected ones that can really knock you for a loop. They can make you question your life choices and your day-to-day lifestyle.

Nothing is harder than facing mortality. A parent, a spouse, a child, a close friend, a relative, or a boss. Any one can die in a second, and you are forever changed when that happens. Other major life events—divorce, job loss, serious illness, a new baby, marriage, graduation—all can be the impetus for soul searching that forces a person to reevaluate what matters most, set new goals, and dream new dreams.

Every one of us takes life for granted. That is until fate, or we ourselves, intervene. Many of us live in the comfortable illusion that our life will go on forever. We squander so many days of our precious existence. We fail to recognize how vulnerable we are until the unexpected happens. Then we tend to step back and assess who we are, what we've done, what truly matters, and what we'd still like to accomplish.

Fact: The past is history and cannot be changed. The future is pure fantasy. Now is all that matters.

Your life is made up of choices. You control the job you have, the amount of success you experience, where you live, who your friends are, and what you do. You control your relationships, your attitudes, and your goals. *You are the architect of your life and only you can plan it, improve it, and make it more fulfilling.* We all know this but too often we forget to act on it.

Let me encourage you that right now *is* the time to take a long, hard look at what's most important to you, and what it is that will make you truly happy. Relish being you! Be the best person possible. Go ahead, flaunt *Brand You*—you are special. Let the world know it.

What neither you, nor I, control is how much time we have left on this planet. I've done my best to encourage you to live a happy life. To be the best you, you can be. To rejoice in the uniqueness of who you are. To let the inner you radiate for all to see. Do not devalue yourself and critique yourself too harshly. Instead, see the unique special gem of a person that is you.

Follow your passions and live the life you want. Live this new philosophy that emphasizes and builds your career on your strengths and your natural gifts. If you follow this advice you should enjoy a very rewarding career that offers just about anything you can dream. Many others have succeeded by following this road map, so why not you? It's a surefire formula for you to achieve happiness.

MORE CAREER RESOURCES
TO AID YOU

obin's advice and articles continuously appear in magazines and newspapers, and her monthly e-newsletter offers motivating articles, tips, and career advice. Let Robin keep your career on track with her free e-newsletter. Sign up at www.RobinRyan.com.

Robin wants to continue to coach you to fulfill your dreams. She'll send you a free gift, her new audio CD *Yes, You Can Achieve Great Success.* To get a copy, mail your name, postal address, email, and a $5 check for shipping and handling to: Robin Ryan's Success CD, 14404 SE 93rd Street, Newcastle, WA 98059, and your CD will immediately be in the mail.

Robin Ryan has authored other popular books and audio training programs that are valuable aids in the career management process. Her books, available in bookstores and on her website, include: *60 Seconds & You're Hired!*, which provides comprehensive job interview and salary negotiation strategies; *Winning Resumes*, **2nd Edition**; *Winning Cover Letters*, **second edition**; and *What to Do with the Rest of Your Life*, which is a valuable roadmap for changing your career and improving your life!

Her popular audio and computer training programs, found at www.RobinRyan.com, include: *The Brand You Kit; Salary Negotiation Strategies; The DreamMaker*, her motivating career-changing program; *The Stand Out Resumes & Cover Letters Creation Kit;* and *Interview Advantage,* which contains information to help you prepare and excel in job interviews.

Robin Ryan has spent a lifetime dedicated to helping people advance their careers. A licensed vocational counselor for more than twenty years, she has an active career counseling practice where she offers in-person and telephone consultations to assist a nationwide list of clients with developing *Brand You*, promotions, resumés and cover letters, interviews, salary negotiation, career changes, and other issues. Her personal goal for each of her clients is that they win a great job they love and are well paid for their efforts. Check her website for specific services that may help you.

Robin is a popular *national speaker;* check her website for a listing of live keynotes, workshops, teleseminars, and webinars in which you can participate.

Contact Robin Ryan at her Seattle office at **425.226.0414**
Email her at robinryan@aol.com
Visit her website at: **www.RobinRyan.com**